Acclaim for
Love, Loss, and Awakening

DENNIS FREED'S *Love, Loss, and Awakening: (Mis)adventures on the Way Back to Joy* is an engaging story of how one man bounces back after losing the love of his life. It is an ode to the power of being in Relationship especially when faced with incredibly difficult and heartbreaking loss. And it is with much humor that Freed takes the reader on a journey to find what we are all looking for; to be joyous and fulfilled in Relationship.

> — Harville Hendrix, Ph.D. And Helen LaKelly Hunt, Ph.D.
> Co-creators of Imago Therapy and authors of
> New York Times bestseller *Getting the Love You Want*

"THIS IS A STORY of digging deep after loss to find that being with another is still worth the risk, staying open to lessons both human and Divine. At times an excruciating memoir of living with cancer, at others, a combination of 'How To' and, more useful, 'How NOT To' of middle-aged dating. Those who have loved deeply will be reminded of what they have and have lost. For others, it's a promise of how good a relationship can be. It has a happy ending, yet acknowledges that seeking love must always include a willingness to lose again."

> —Cynthia Wall, LCSW, author of *The Courage to Trust:*
> *A Guide to Building Deep and Lasting Relationships*

"GET READY TO CRY, laugh, cringe, and howl with wonder and delight as you go through Dennis Freed's amazing experiences after the loss of his wife. He offers heartfelt real-life insights on how to cope with the despair and overcome the pain so you can face the world and find love and happiness anew."

> —Paul J. Krupin, author of *Words People Love to Hear –*
> *Simple Verbal Recipes for Making the People Around You Feel Good*

Love, Loss,
and
Awakening

*(Mis)adventures
on the Way Back to Joy*

Dennis P. Freed

Mark & Sue
Love is a never ending
adventure. Thank you for
the support of our kids.
Love

TOLAWAKEN
PRESS

LOVE, LOSS, AND AWAKENING
(Mis)adventures on the Way Back to Joy
Copyright © 2016 Dennis P. Freed

TOLAWAKEN PRESS
523 Manhattan Avenue, Unit 2
New York, NY 10027
www.lovelossandawakening.com

Book production and design by Cypress House
Cover image: © Romolo Tavani - Fotolia.com
Interior photo credits courtesy of the author's archives

PUBLISHER'S CATALOGING-IN-PUBLICATION DATA

Names: Freed, Dennis P., author.

Title: Love, loss, and awakening : (mis)adventures on the way back to joy / Dennis P. Freed.

Description: First edition. | New York, NY : Tolawaken Press, [2016]

Identifiers: ISBN: 978-0-9971916-1-5 (paperback) | 978-0-9971916-3-9 (hardcover) | 978-0-9971916-2-2 (ebook) | LCCN: 2016931395

Subjects: LCSH: Widowers--United States--Biography. | Spouses--Death--Psychological aspects. | Cancer--Patients--Family relationships. | Cancer--Patients--Biography. | Married people--Psychological aspects. | Grief. | Bereavement. | Loss (Psychology) | Dating (Social customs) | Mate selection. | Widowers--Life skills guides.

Classification: LCC: HQ1058.5.U5 F74 2016 | DDC: 306.88/20973--dc23

PRINTED IN THE USA
2 4 6 8 9 7 5 3 1

I have recreated events, locales, and conversations from my memories of them. I have changed the names of several individuals and places in order to protect their privacy, and in some instances I may have changed identifying characteristics and details such as physical properties, occupations, and places of residence. All opinions expressed in this book are my own.

*"Every joyous minute lost with your best friend, lover
and spouse is a minute never to be seen again.
Sometimes tomorrow just never comes."*

Dennis Freed

"I Love You, Denny."

Hope Freed

*"Is there a God?" "Is there something else after we die?"
"Is our deceased loved one really watching over us?"*
Everyone one of us!

I DEDICATE THIS BOOK to four people, one-hundred-plus women, and a single rabbi.

MY LATE WIFE AND LOVE for thirty-two years, Hope Freed, without whose kind, humorous, and childlike exploration of the world I would be nothing but a selfish, unhappy man.

MY PARENTS, Babette and Mel, and in-laws, Harriet and Bernie. From them, my children and I gained insight into what it's like to grow old together. I list each couple as one because they truly are one. Marriage isn't constant joy but an understanding that it could be worse, and that it gets better every day because you can kiss each other good morning.

MY NEW FRIEND JOAN MARANS DIM. We are widow and widower. We stumble around our new life together, helping each other realize we were blessed once and will not settle for anything less than a future of smiles.

THE HUNDRED-PLUS WOMEN I DATED, interviewed, met for coffee, and frolicked with. I sincerely apologize for the mistakes I made, and I thank you deeply for the sometimes not-too-pleasant lessons you taught me. We all were just trying to survive, find a soul mate, and achieve an end to a single life imposed willfully or unwillingly upon ourselves.

AND TO THE RABBI: "You'll just have to read the book to find out."

Contents

Preface

I AWOKE AT 4:00 AM and could not get back to sleep. As is commonplace in our society, I reached for my iPhone to read my emails. An email from a dear friend, Joan, rested in my inbox. Joan and I shared the last year together, not as lovers but as widow and widower friends trying to survive a new life without our best friends, lifetime guides, and confidants—our deceased spouses. I was reluctant to read the email. Joan and I had been through so much together, and at 4:00 AM. I wasn't sure I wanted to start my day in the history-hell of remembrances.

After reading Joan's email I cried a deep cry of gratefulness. Together we survived the mercurial mental onslaught of a widow and widower's inaugural months and years. We both refused to accept a fate mired in sadness as we shared our lives and deepest, most secret histories in an attempt to regain a foothold in joy. We both were finally accepting our deceased spouses' approval to live a new life without them.

Prior to Hope's death, I didn't fully comprehend the power of "The Dark Night of the Soul."* After her death, "The Dark Night of the Soul" followed me, played peek-a-boo with me, and led me for

---

* From the sixteenth-century poem by Saint John of the Cross, which has numerous interpretations. It is a powerful journey within oneself when adversity greets your life. It can be related to one's reunion with Divinity or to a non-religious interpretation of the ability to overcome extreme adversity and the new person that emerges from that struggle.

a spell until I was liberated. But, like Lucifer himself, that night eventually vanished into the dark realms whence it came. My soul and mind were purged and were ready for the next phase. *Love, Loss, and Awakening* embraces many of my struggles as I emerged from the bloated physical and mental sadness.

As the next chapter of my life unfolded, so did the many questions of Divinity, our purpose in life, and what awaits after our human form ceases to exist. I originally started to write *Love, Loss, and Awakening* as a cathartic memoir, but so much more evolved as my pen touched the page. Divinity became a guiding question.

I like to reference life through examples. Two films illustrate the essence of this book: *Blade Runner* and *The Adjustment Bureau*. *Blade Runner has* long been on my all-time top-five list. The ending scene with Deckard and Roy Batty, the antagonist in *Blade Runner*, fighting to the death, and then the paradoxical saving of life, has weighed heavily in my thoughts. I share it with you to better understand *Love, Loss, and Awakening*. We all wonder about life and death, but a person who has lost a soul mate, someone he shared a bed with for decades, finds that question tearing at him throughout the next part of his life. How do we accept this death and not dishonor the departed if we think they are looking over us? Was there a Divine purpose for their life with us as well as their death?

As Batty's life ends he compares it with tears lost in a rainstorm. Will all those amazing sights he witnessed really be lost like tears in rain? Each raindrop gives birth to a new beginning, eventually evaporating to start the life cycle over again. Is this our existence? Did our spouse die only to water a new cycle of life?

Deckard watches as the dying Batty contemplates his preprogrammed brief life span. We watch each other die, too. With each deathwatch, questions trouble the very fabric of our existence—how much longer have we got, and how are we to live this life? Each deathwatch ultimately ends with our own questions: "What's next for me?" "Is my behavior on this earth being watched and judged?" "Is there a master plan?"

As for the importance of *The Adjustment Bureau*, I was alone in my home in Massachusetts recently going through some inner turmoil. I have one of those televisions with all the Bose System wires and connections only an aerospace engineer can trace to fix a problem. The TV went on the fritz and the screen looked like a version of the old TV show *Outer Limits*. If you're under the age of forty-five you've probably not seen the show, but the screen was all scrambled as if taken over by aliens. Anyway, after I'd fumbled with the wires for about ten minutes, the mayhem stopped and the DVD went on. Playing was the final scene of *The Adjustment Bureau*. At exactly that moment, I really needed the reassurance "that all will be fine and trust in the Divine." Was that coincidence or was it a message sent to me? As it turned out, my inner turmoil was self-doubt, and everything was as it should be.

Love, Loss, and Awakening is a compilation of vignettes that parallel not only my life but also the lives of those who traveled with me. I started writing it one year after Hope's death. The first chapters were "Hope" and "Her Tear." As the years of my widower's life progressed, future chapters emerged, culminating almost four years after Hope's death. Let's journey together through sadness and laughter, through pain and pleasure, through loss and discovery as you read *Love, Loss, and Awakening*.

Dennis

January 2016

Introduction

BEING A LONG-TERM CAREGIVER to your spouse differs from other types of caregiving: Your caregiving for your spouse parallels the caregiving for a child or elderly parent. Partnership intimacy fades as the illness expands. Conversations about the future diminish as you witness your partner dying and notice the seething regret in their eyes. You need to choose your words carefully, as if you were speaking to your children. As your role takes on new meaning, so does your devotion. Your love grows on many different levels—as that of a spouse, best friend, and now parent. You find yourself making decisions with all those roles to consider.

And one day your spouse, lover, and very best friend dies. After decades, you're alone to figure out your future on your own. No best-trusted friend to bounce ideas off of; no best-trusted friend to help pick up the pieces of a decision gone awry. Friends and relatives can't understand the emptiness unless they also are widows or widowers. Even then, their relationship was not yours, for no two relationships are alike. The road to a new future is individual and constantly changing as the new and varying experiences multiply. Your past way of life and your morals and opinions are constantly trying to find the serenity that has left you. Your children, parents, and friends are constantly questioning and unwelcoming, invading this new life you stumble around in. The peace of familiarity is replaced with uncertainty. What new inner peace will you find?

Damn it—my Best Friend just died! What the hell am I to do? But as the journey unfolds there is always one friend who's there 24/7 as you weave a new life. That friend always listens, never speaks unless asked for direction, and their words of wisdom, though never audible, are clearly understood.

Chapter One

Hope

I WAS ON AN interesting date. She was an attractive, petite, intelligent woman, and roughly ten years younger than I. She was the perfect image of my next spouse. We all have images of whom we will marry or, if married, whom we'd want to marry if we had to do it again. Dreaming is so much fun without real-life consequences.

With much in common we talked for hours. I focused on her pleasing steel-blue eyes and our delightful conversation as we sipped our chardonnay at the boutique Italian restaurant in Hell's Kitchen in Manhattan. The atmosphere was splendid. Aged brick walls, hammered-tin ceilings, and low-level music surrounded us. Everything was going well.

Twice during dinner my companion pulled out lip gloss and redecorated her lips with that fine kissing coating—an indication, I hoped, that she liked me, wanted a goodnight kiss or more, and would see me again, but then she asked me a question that turned into a fatal dating error:

"What was the best thing you ever did in your life?" she asked.

"Do you want my real answer?" I asked.

"Of course," she said.

"Marrying my wife, Hope, at twenty-three," I said.

The look in her eyes changed ever so slightly from pleasant to inquisitive, and I hoped my reply appeared loving. Instead it seemed to put her on the defensive. Maybe she was wondering if she could ever measure up, or if I was truly over my wife's death. Then I buried the hatchet (in myself) and added: "I married a Rolls Royce, and one day I will find a Bentley."

"I see," she said in a tone that made clear this date was over and all my lustful imaginings would never be realized.

A friend of mine later told me that women find such a statement offensive—never compare a woman to a car.

After each date, you see, a widower must master a new self-control and learn what he can and cannot say. For decades, as a husband, I always replied honestly to whatever Hope asked, without thinking about consequences. That doesn't mean my responses were always pleasing or correct, but Hope always knew I meant well and accepted my apologies. Not so with a date. I probably should have known that, but if I had said this to my Hope she would have shrugged it off, informed me it was offensive, and then accepted me for me. Such mistakes aren't tolerated in the dating game, however, so the second date never occurred. Shortly thereafter the attractive woman sent me an email saying I was not her type. She wished me well and hoped I'd find my Bentley.

Another lesson learned without Hope to guide me. My wife was my conscience, you see. She would pull me back from my excesses or tactfully let me know when I'd made an inappropriate comment. I'm on my own now and must be my own conscience and regulator. My wife and I had unbroken trust and knew unquestionably that we would never intentionally harm each other. Oh, how I miss that unconditional trust, sharing mistakes that are understood as unintentional, and the general understanding that we would not hurt one another. Speaking to my peers who are widows or widowers, this is a common essential piece missing in our lives—something we took for granted and now long for so dearly.

Still, I am learning after more than a year and a half years of being a widower that I had an amazing marriage. Mainly because of Hope's character, our marriage steadily grew over the thirty-one years we lived together. Hope was a gifted woman, and I was lucky to be married to her. She hadn't taken the prescribed path upon graduating high school. She traveled and worked all over the United States, Egypt, and Israel until she was twenty-one, learning life as she unraveled it.

It was her travels and mine that cemented us together in our first meeting at a Halloween party at our town's local disco. I had graduated from college five months before. Neither of us liked disco, but friends urged us to go that night. We both grew up in Oceanside, New York, and went to the same elementary, junior high, and high schools, so we had many mutual friends.

Hope was a year younger than I and always popular. I wasn't. I was shy around girls. The other boys hung around that cute little red-haired girl named Hope. Our paths crossed sometimes, but we never spoke to each other before that Halloween night. After our first meeting we began to fall in love immediately. My parents tell me I came home from the party, woke them up, and said, "I think I found the girl I'll marry."

Two and a half months later, Hope and I were engaged. Ten months after that, we were married. We bought our first and only home a year after we wed. After six years, and many travels around the U.S. and Europe, we started our family. April 7, 2012, almost thirty-two years after we first met that night, Hope died in the only house we ever called home.

Hope was stunningly beautiful, inside and out. As my neighbor often said, "You could strike a match off her cute little body." She had pleasing red hair, not the kind that was bright orange but the kind that movie actresses toss around. She loved to dress funky, and clothes and playful accessories were her hobby and passion. Her clothes only further graced her frame and personality. After Hope's death from cancer, one of her coworkers said, "Every morning we would wait to see how Hope dressed. We all knew we could try to copy her, but no one graced the style like she did."

Hope's smile could melt any ill intention, and her soft, soothing voice could calm us in the worst of times. Her knack for making you feel at ease with her choice of words, coupled with her unwavering patience, made her an exceptional educator and a person others sought out for advice. Her personality made you feel comfortable, like wearing your favorite pajamas. Later in her career she used these personality traits to help thousands of people live better lives. Hope's personality, combined with her undaunted seven years of courage to fight cancer, served as an example to many that they too could beat life's difficulties.

Hope's quest to live and share with others was buttressed by her reading, learning, and implementing every New Age holistic concept (food, meditation, sound therapy, qigong, psychological, social) she could lay her hands on. These soothing, educational, sharing, and endearingly comfortable attributes earned her the nickname "Hopey," which fit perfectly. She was all our "Hopey." After Hope and I had been married a year, my mother convinced Hope to become a teacher. She embraced this vocation with her entire soul. She became a kindergarten teacher, and the students adored her. They called her Ms. Hope.

An innovator in the classroom, Hope cultivated the kids' love of learning. She taught them mental stillness, meditation, and qigong, a Chinese holistic system of wellness, many years before these practices became widely known or accepted. When she taught art she didn't just have her students paint. Oh, no, she taped brown paper under their desks and had them lie on their backs to paint like Michelangelo—just as he painted the Sistine Chapel. Real fun was when she taught the kids about the abstract art of Jackson Pollack, and they flung paint onto their canvases. Valentine's Day was always a special treat: Hope would bring a real cow heart into the classroom and the five-year-olds would dissect it together, exploring not only the heart but also the wonders of Hope's imaginative teaching.

This was Hope, to live and learn the way she wished she had. As a kid she wasn't considered a good student; she was bored and didn't find learning fun. The cycle of boredom reinforced the school's concept of her abilities, and she was channeled down the path of mediocrity. Later, as a teacher, Hope refused to make the same mistake. She chose to focus on every student's interest so each could find learning fun and exciting. No student of hers was to ever leave class—as she had often done when she was a child—without the chance to excel in what they did best.

When Hope died, *Newsday,* the local Long Island, New York, newspaper, printed an article about her and how she'd touched so many lives. This was a testament to our dear and beloved "Hopey." She was truly an angel and a messenger from the Divine. To validate this, she died Passover evening in the United States and Easter in Israel. She was a Divine gift lent to this world for a brief time.

Hope and I did have our difficult years. We had two boys, Evan and Ryan. Hope was a calming and loving mother, sometimes too calming. I was always the major disciplinarian because it was against Hope's nature to administer tough love to growing boys. About twenty-one years into our marriage we hit a real rough patch. Travel, ice hockey, and the rigors of raising kids tore at our once happy marriage. We fell out of love for about two years, but raising our children kept us together.

I must sidetrack first to a conversation I struck up with a manager of a Costco store in Springfield, Massachusetts, while picking up groceries and paper goods for the one-year anniversary dinner of Hope's death. Springfield is close to my second home in the Berkshire Mountains, and thirty people were coming up for the anniversary. Hope had been cremated. Her last wishes were that we spread her ashes into the lake our Massachusetts home overlooked. I could not bring myself to heed her wishes until the anniversary and was dreading the weekend.

I was alone in Costco and in an extremely depressed, introspective mood. The store manager proved to be a loving, empathetic woman, and noticed my demeanor. She initiated a conversation with a warm smile that allowed my innermost feelings to pour out. She too had been married for more than thirty years, and as I told her the story of my life with Hope, she intertwined her marriage experiences with mine and shared a profound perception that long-time married couples can really appreciate.

"Every great marriage has a moment when a couple decides whether they stick it out," she said. "It's the couples who stick it out and then work hard at their marriage that develop a deep, everlasting love."

She was right. Hope and I had our difficult moments during those two years, and one morning we almost ended it. It was 5:30 AM and I was crying in the bathroom, getting ready for work, knowing instinctively that our marriage had failed. Hope still lay in bed. I walked into the bedroom and she was propped up looking at me with a face I had never seen before. It was one of terror and concern, not terror of being physically hurt but terror of losing all she had worked so hard for. We stared at each other, and she started to cry too.

I said, "Do we end this?"

She was now in total control to make our decision. Her words, her answer, was so classically simple Hopey: "No, Denny, let's make this work." Denny was the nickname she used for me when we were happy and playing.

We hugged and kissed like people who didn't want to leave each other, ever. The fear of never kissing again embraced each kiss and hug. After that morning, our marriage grew to one of love and understanding, getting better with each passing year. We spent more time together and worked at making our union special. We went to quite a few marriage seminars and New Age courses. Hope's holistic learning became my quest too. She cultivated the soft psychological knowledge and I the more scientific avenues. We found a new common core to explore as a married couple, and as we did, we constantly questioned our understanding of Divinity. We shared what we learned and applied it to making our marriage better. Often it was the smallest touches that made the biggest difference.

In the mornings, before work, we left each other little love notes on the kitchen table, or tucked in our clothes, work knapsacks, and travel bags. The notes ranged from simple, hand-drawn smiley faces to details of why we loved each other so much. On occasion I would even find a note in my smelly hockey gloves as I put them on to play late at night or in my boots on ski trips thousands of miles away, which made me feel close to home.

In addition to these love notes, my wife would mail to my workplace cards with famous sonnets and phrases. I sent flowers to her kindergarten class at least twice a month, with love notes attached. Hope loved sunflowers, and when available they adorned her desk to brighten up her classroom, her students, and her day. When I cleaned out the home after her death, I found, in several files, every note we'd ever penned—hundreds, maybe thousands of them. They showed that we'd learned to enjoy being together again and cherish each other as we had during the first decades of our marriage. We never wanted to repeat that morning of decision, and we never did.

That was long ago. Now, after dating more than a hundred women and hearing their tales, I know I was the luckiest man alive. Hope and I argued, but we learned to reduce our arguments to a trickle and to no more than fifteen minutes' duration. Time spent away from each other turned into more time together as we grew our love and marriage. Our sex life, when Hope wasn't sick, was creative. I know from my dating experiences that many women have never explored an iota of what Hope and I shared. I'm learning that our married life was wonderful. I won't share the details, out of respect for my wife, but even at intimacy we strived to improve our love. Let's just say Chinese food in the bathtub could be a prelude to an evening's delight. I truly was blessed, and only after losing my best friend and lover am I learning how wonderful life was.

I'll share one more story of our deep love for each other. Hope was being wheeled on a gurney from the ER to her hospital room. She was a constant inpatient during the last years of her life. The orderly who was assigned to us greeted us with an understanding of how much we loved each other. He had wheeled Hope down the winding corridors before. He said, drawn out and full of endearment, "Hi, Mr. and Mrs. Freed. I hope someday I can obtain the love you two have for each other. It's so rare and special. I just had to share this with you."

This man confirmed, without a doubt, that Hope and I had lived with true love so often described in novels, sonnets, and movies. When Hope finally passed, my life fell into an abyss. Several months later, a dear friend of Hope's and mine since childhood, who was only fifty-three, developed stage IV cancer. Instead of letting this push me further into despair, I decided to live every day to the fullest. I started to date, travel, and run away from the memories. I wanted sex again after so many years of abstinence. And I wanted "it"—true Divine love—again. The yearning for true love, which includes undeniable loyalty and trust, is one of the hardest things to be denied for widows and widowers who had a happy marriage. I'm lucky to have widow and widower friends who've found true love again; they're my role models. In fact I'm the luckiest man alive. I had Hope, who prepared me for this new journey by sharing her optimism, knowledge, happy disposition, and view of life as a simple pleasure to be cherished.

I made many sad and laughable mistakes. I hit bottom and slowly clawed my way out of the abyss to a new life—one without Hope. I wrote this book to help my healing as a widower. The book portrays my quest for a new best friend as well as my mistakes, anecdotes of lessons learned, and experiences along the way. I share many of these experiences in later chapters. Please laugh and cry with me on my journey.

In future, if I'm asked the question: "What was the best thing you ever did?" my answer will differ slightly from my earlier reply. I'll say: "Finding my first best friend and lover at twenty-two—and then finding a new and different best friend and lover a second time." Maybe by the time this book is published she will be by my side; if not, I know she's waiting for me to find her.

Hope preparing for a new wig after more than 250 chemotherapy treatments. This is how she would want to be remembered. She learned to be fearless, and every challenge was a new beginning for a positive future.

April 9, 2012
Hope's Obituary Picture in
Newsday newspaper

Chapter Two

The Rabbi

FIVE YEARS BEFORE HOPE'S death her cancer came back with a vengeance. The ominous part was the cancer had lodged deep in her abdomen, next to the spine. The surgery Hope was about to undergo was difficult: Her stomach and surrounding organs had to be removed to get to the cancer. At the time there was no other method to treat it. We agreed to the operation knowing how dire her situation was. Stage IV cancer treatment is very risky, and Hope suffered a complication: There was a tear in her intestine. A massive infection spread throughout her already weakened body. For three months she fought the infection like a soldier— a stalemate with no side winning or losing but carnage mounting in her body.

Death did not win and neither did health. At its height, the infection produced an unbelievable scene: One day as the doctors were inspecting Hope, a boil slowly developed on her abdomen. Brimming with pus, it grew like a volcano waiting to explode. And that is what occurred. The boil grew and grew in front of us as we watched in disbelief. The doctors were as spellbound as we were watching the skin rise and stretch, and then it broke, spewing ounces of infection in rhythm with Hope's heartbeat. How our body tries to heal is amazing.

The next day, my father came to relieve me for a few hours. We all felt death was near. I was physically and mentally exhausted, I needed the rest. As I walked out of the hospital room I noticed an Orthodox rabbi dressed in his classic long robe and wide-brimmed hat, with *tzitzit* (ceremonial tassels) showing below his inner jacket. At this time in life I had become an agnostic, perhaps even an atheist. I'd lost all belief in Divinity. How could a wonderful woman like Hope be made to endure the constant torture of this horrific ordeal *There could be no Divine that would permit this,* I thought.

With the tired, worn soul only a long-term intensive caregiver wears, I approached the rabbi. He instinctively understood my mental and physical predicament, delicately accepted my approach, and offered the comfort that only a man of the cloth can provide. I broke down in uncontrollable tears, and said, "How can there be a G-d who is making my wife suffer so much? I used to believe in Him so faithfully, but now I feel He doesn't exist."

The rabbi responded with a parable I don't remember clearly, but I do recall his final words of Divine wisdom: "G-d has a plan and one day you will understand it. There will be signs and unexplainable coincidences. Once you recognize and acknowledge them you will know He exists and there is a purpose."

Hope survived that three-month ordeal. She left the hospital weighing ninety-six pounds, frail but alive and full of belief that she would live to see her grandchildren. I shared the rabbi's words with her. Over the next several years of her illness the signs started to multiply and our understanding and belief in the Divine returned. After Hope's death the signs continued, including her visitations to me and to her closest friends and relatives. Hope died believing there was more than this human existence; the smile on her face as she took her last breath was the evidence.

Chapter Three

One Big Happy Family

From September to mid-December 2011 there occurred our family's most memorable times. It was those last few months before Hope's fast decline that are so valuable to us. It's truly remarkable how an intimate tragedy can coalesce into a warm, memorable experience.

By mid-August, Hope's cancer had entered her right thighbone, extremely rare for ovarian cancer. The chances of survival for her and our partnership were waning. The Divine seems to sense when further intervention is required. A week or so after Hope's cancer entered her bones my work life was shattered. I was a principal in an international construction company, running one of the largest, if not the largest, residential divisions in the United States. We had new management, and many of my executive peers had left the company by this time. I was one of the last few remaining executives from the old regime, and I didn't entirely fit in with the new management's outlook. A situation occurred with one of my superiors that devastated my view of my entire career. My understanding of human nature had been dismantled, and that, coupled with Hope's recent medical situation, shattered me. Due to all the pressures, I had a mental lapse for the first time in my business career, and should probably have handled the situation differently, but the affliction was emotionally devastating. And then the Divine intervened.

One of my peers walked into my office and closed the door. He understood my anguish, and as tears of empathy streamed down his cheeks, he said, "Leave. Get out of here now."

A widower whose wife had died from cancer, he had worked during his wife's illness. He repeated, "Leave or you'll regret not spending this time with your wife for the rest of your life. Trust me—I suffer every day for not leaving work sooner."

Those words hounded me over the course of the next two weeks. Without my knowledge, The Divine paved a path for me to be able to enjoy several months of family bliss. By mid-September, I left the company I had worked in for eighteen years, to be with my entire family for the last time with absolutely no working-world worries.

All Divine cylinders drove the engineering of these months to come. My older son, Evan, had graduated college and was living at home with us. He was at Hope's and my side. Hope and Evan were extremely close, and his presence comforted her as the ordeal took its course. Evan's closest friend was his younger brother Ryan. Together they formed a formidable defensive pair in ice hockey, Evan on defense and Ryan in goal. In business, since Ryan's ninth grade, they competed around the country in DECA, a high school club that prepares emerging leaders and entrepreneurs for their future careers. Through Hope's illness the two comforted each other even as one medical episode after another exploded into difficulty.

Ryan was missing from the equation to make us whole as a family. He was entering his senior year at the University of Minnesota. Ryan is exceedingly creative in finding ways to achieve the outcomes he seeks. He wanted to join us and complete the family. Somehow, he found a way to conduct his classes for the semester in our home in Oceanside, Long Island.

Our family was entirely together, and one more addition was to join us. Evan had fallen in love with a delightfully cheery and beautiful woman who had a propensity to liven up any occasion. Somehow sadness always disappeared when Lindsay was around, and Lindsay became part of our home.* She moved in to be with us and support us in that delightful September. The hand of G-d works in mysterious ways and knits a world we sometimes just don't understand at the moment.

Our home was full with our children at our side, not as receptors of our guidance but as adult friends. Every evening we all ate dinner together and discussions took on new laughter and understanding. We were sharing our lives as equals. Every two weeks, Hope received her chemotherapy treatment and was incapacitated for several days. She didn't want to be left out of the daily fracas, so our living room couch became her place of fulfillment. Her pillows and comforters adorned the couch as she lay there watching us. When well, she interjected her own brand of humor.

The kitchen had a thirteen-inch TV on a wall-mounted swivel, and was a good fourteen feet from the couch. The entire family would sit next to Hope, squinting as we watched her favorite shows: *Everybody Loves Raymond, Two and Half Men,* and *I Love Lucy.* We must have watched every episode at least three times, but we laughed at each one as if seeing it for the first time. Only comedy programs could be played when Hope was around. She filled her life with happiness as she strove to get better. That couch is filled with memorable stories; I'll share one with you.

Hope needed to smoke marijuana to endure the intense chemotherapy regimen. She tried everything and pot was the only thing that would relax the stomach-wrenching spasms so she could eat

---

* The November after Hope's death, Lindsay and Evan became engaged at the Wishing Well in the Magic Kingdom in Disney World, one of Hope's favorite places. Lindsay's parents, Ryan, and I hid in the bushes and witnessed Evan's proposal to Lindsay. They were married the next fall. Hope was not physically present, but the ceiling lights shone bright in the wedding hall.

just enough to survive the treatments. One night Evan entered the living room with one of those T-Shirts with the words and letters all jumbled. Lindsay, Ryan, and I tried to make sense of the scrambled words as Hope dozed off from her recent marijuana treatment. Then she woke up and asked what was going on, just as a napping five-year-old might when not wanting to be left out of the happenings of the world. As we explained what we were trying to do, her marijuana-lucid mind said, "Oh, come on, that's easy." She then, without pause, deciphered the jumbled words. We all laughed uncontrollably as the three of us recalled similar college incidents of pot-inspired revelations. Hope caught on and joined in our glee.

Ryan and I formed a bond that will be everlasting. He was home with me every day. We shared the medical chores and daily home regimen, but the true bonding occurred every morning when we would work out in our basement home gym and then meditate together. This daily physical and mindfulness exercise had a lasting impact and is reflected in Ryan's current entrepreneurial endeavor.

At night, Evan, Ryan, and I would sit together in the hot tub and relax our exhausted minds and muscles while Lindsay and Hope bonded. Though she never expressed it outwardly, I feel that Hope had a belief even that her chances of seeing Lindsay and Evan married were slim. She wanted to know everything about Lindsay so she could feel certain that Evan would be graced with a caring, loving woman. Lindsay and Hope laughed, cried, and shared lives. They became mother and daughter, and it was a true gift that they could experience each other. Length of time doesn't always equate with quality, and the compression of time can bring joys that long duration sometimes can't fulfill.

The weeks passed and our family grew to new understandings. There was a feeling of encouragement with each chemotherapy treatment. We were becoming a family of five now, and Hope so much wanted the future. She decided she was going to surprise us with a family vacation. This was the only time all of us would travel together as a family. Hope picked a luxurious vacation spa in Pennsylvania. For four days and nights we ate all our meals together, played together, and had fun together. Hope's strength had diminished and she couldn't accompany us on a hike into the mountains. Cheerfully, she told us to go without her and occupied her time with spa amenities. This was our last family vacation, but one none of us will ever forget.

In early December, Hope and I decided to go on a vacation to Disney World, which was becoming our vacation spot for many reasons: First and foremost was that Orlando International Airport was just a two-hour flight from New York City, with lots of flights available should we have to scurry back to NYC if medical needs required. In addition to location, Disney World was extremely handicap friendly and accessible. They made Hope feel special, as they could see on her face the effects of chemotherapy. Disney World also sported many fine restaurants and lots of fun entertainment. Hope loved the shows in all the parks—they were happy and upbeat, and laughter and children were what she wanted to be surrounded with.

During this vacation Hope was extremely weak and for the first time needed a wheelchair. We checked in and the chair was brought out to us. I started to cry uncontrollably, the gravity of her illness sinking in like never before, but Hope wasn't going to let a wheelchair affect her one bit. She looked at me crying, and then at the chair. "Oh, so much fun," she said, grinning like a child. "You will be my driver, and I can order you around as I wish."

And so she did. We would travel through the parks mimicking Mr. Toad's Magic Ride, making errant turns and hitting walls with the kind of playfulness children use when parents aren't looking. Hope was living her kindergarten classroom experiences in that wheelchair.

I want to share two events that come to mind from that trip. One involved the famous actor Edward James Olmos. As we waited in the handicap queuing area for one of the Magic Kingdom shows, he happened to walk in next to us. I thanked him for his wonderful entertainment (coincidentally, he had co-starred in *Blade Runner*). He looked at Hope and recognized her situation. Politely, he asked if we would like a photo of the two of us with him. He embraced Hope in her wheelchair and placed his arm on the chair's handrail as if he was a dear friend. The photo was snapped. Oh, Hope's smile in that picture is childlike, and here it is.

Hope and Dennis
with Edward James Olmos at Disney World.

Hope so much wanted to be or be surrounded with children, which brings us to the next story. We loved watching the nighttime Electric Light Parade in the Magic Kingdom. It's truly magical. The Disney-character floats are all brightly lit in colorful LEDs as the characters stroll on the fringes and favorite Disney tunes fill the night air. We were in the handicap section and got an early seat on the curb of the street, a prime viewing location. The curb was packed with onlookers waiting for the parade to begin. I felt a tap on my shoulder, and a grandparent behind us asked if we could make room for their five-year-old grandson. I don't know how, but the boy made his way between Hope and me. As the parade began, the three of us acted as if we were friends from home, laughing, giggling, and greeting the Disney characters. At one point Hope and the boy started to wave to the characters and call for them to come over. The waving turned into childlike beckoning of each character by name as Hope and the boy wanted so much to be recognized by them.

"Hey, Peter. Hi, Goofy. I love you, Donald."

I joined in the fun, and the three of us were chums who collected badges of honor as, one by one, the characters shook our hands. The parade ended and we parted just as friends say goodnight when it's time to go home after a summer night's game of tag. Hope had a child's or maybe a grandmother's smile on her face. It was the grandmother she wanted to be. A week after we came home her illness took a severe nosedive and we never laughed again as a couple.

I don't want to end this chapter on a sad note. Those last few months before Hope became a permanent resident in the hospital were filled with joy and delightful memories. How many people have moments that are so clear and enjoyable? How many adults can say they spent months living with their adult children without cares and only fun? How many adults in their fifties have played with a parade or made a crazy go-cart out of a wheelchair? How many adults surrounded themselves with only comedies every night?

Yes, Hope was going to die, but her teachings, laughter, childlike outlook, and love will remain with my family, friends, and her students forever. How many adults can say they experienced, laughed with, lived with, and deeply loved Hope Freed for thirty-two years?

I can, and that graces my journey every single day.

Chapter Four

Her Tear

FOR FOUR LONG DAYS my wife, Hope, lay cocooned in her body. Excessive calcium in her blood, caused by cancer eating away at her bones, had shut down every sensory system in her body except for her hearing. The hospice nurse tending to my wife informed me that hearing is the last of the senses to disappear before consciousness is lost. In this state of being, the dying person cannot move a muscle, talk, respond, or function, but hears everything around them vividly.

I remember reading one of my father's Korean War magazines. It described how a soldier who lay bleeding to death was motionless and incapacitated but heard everything. Like my wife, his every sense shut down except for hearing as he lay slowly dying in the snow. He heard all the sounds around him, yet he couldn't summon anyone to save him. Luckily, a medic knew enough to put a mirror to his nose to see if there was any breath. The mirror fogged and the medic immediately gave him plasma. That mirror saved the soldier from death and enabled him to tell his story.

The calcium had shut down Hope's body, and she lay motionless waiting to die. For four days her family and friends visited, our conversations one-directional. How she must have been tormented at being unable to respond. This imprisonment of the mind must feel like being shut in a coffin waiting slowly for the oxygen to run out. My wife was a woman full of vitality and conversation. Now she lay like a frail ghost waiting for her final goodbye. Hope was strong-willed and did not want to let go. She didn't want to die. There was still so much for her to accomplish in life. Hope wanted to teach, she wanted to see her grandchildren, and most of all she wanted to grow old with her best friend. Knowing my wife, she was hoping a miracle cure would come like a knight saving a damsel in the tower keep, but the knight's weapons were now exhausted.

And so the story of her tear began the morning of her death. My entire family was suffering and slowly dying with Hope. Sisters and friends from out of town lost wages and were ravaged by the roller-coaster medical ordeal. The wait for Hope's last breath sapped the life out of the four parents, who were in their own twilight years.

My younger son studying abroad in Europe made the round-trip twice to see his mother, not knowing whether to continue studying or to dismiss an entire semester. Our elder son looked like he was wasting away with anxiety. And then there was I, the seven-year manager of my wife's illness. I had stopped working. I was bloated from stress, eating junk food, and drinking too much alcohol. My life coach and others thought I was going to die first as I rotted my body and mind.

After six months of staying home, I began to work part-time again as a consultant. The hospice specialist urged me to work and keep my mind busy, and so I did—at the price of guilt that nearly two years later still haunted me. I didn't know I would wish back every second I worked those last few weeks of my wife's life. I wanted to work to escape the daily pain, but also because of Hope's newfound abuse of me.

During those last few weeks, she made fun of me, ignored me, and was indifferent to me. This hurt so much. Why didn't anyone tell me it was a standard reaction for a dying person who would never be able to converse, share life moments, or make love with the man she had known best for thirty-two years? It was her way of distancing the pain of losing me. As my soul, mind, and body rotted and the whole family struggled, my wife held on in her cocoon, trying not to leave us.

I often wonder how much reality and fantasy were going on in her entrapped mind. Don't we fantasize in normal life when bored as we wait for a train or bus or stand in line at Disney World? Our fantasies are individual additions to our dreams and desires as we wait for whatever will eventually come. Now imagine dreaming in reality and fantasy as you can't move your body but can hear all around—hours upon hours of thoughts to manipulate. I am sure of one thing: Hope had fantasies that the medical knights were coming to save her. I know this because the hospice specialists told me they'd never seen such will to not let go. I believe this was Hope's foremost thought. I witnessed my wife endure cancer for seven long years, with over three years in the hospital and more than 250 chemo treatments. *They are coming to save me from death,* she must have thought. *I've got so much unfinished business.*

On Saturday morning, April 7th, 2012, one of our closest friends visited me. She came with a piece of new information no one had shared with me. We sat alone in my living room, coffee in hand, and she shared a taboo secret of the type revealed only on the most ominous occasions.

"There is a way to stop Hope's suffering," she said. "We know of others who have been down your path and made the ultimate decision to stop the pain."

Euthanasia was her secret, and as she told it to me tears streamed from her eyes. She loved my wife, and this was the most painful secret to reveal, but she saw the toll on my family and on me and assumed my wife's torment should not go on.

Legally, I can't describe what I learned of the process, but it took many hours to grasp. The details understood, I corralled my two boys. You could see the stress of the last week marking the skin of their young faces. They had wrinkles and odd colors where smooth youthfulness used to be. I sat them down and was about to ask them permission to silence our very best friend forever. My memory of the discussion is cloudy, and I bet if you asked each one of us you would get a different description, like the colors of a rainbow, but the rainbow doesn't always end in a blue sky as it also did not that day.

Together, we made the decision that it was time to stop all the agony. There are no words to convey a decision of such magnitude; only those who have endured a similar conversation can understand the torturous internal debate that culminates in an answer. This is a Divine decision.

With our agreement in our minds, I walked to the bedroom where my wife lay on the bed. She had that gossamer appearance you see so many times in the movies. I sat down and cried like never before. It was a new type of crying, one I'd never experienced. I cried for my kids, I cried for the parents, I cried for my entire family. I cried a cry of goodbye to a woman I'd loved for thirty-two years. Then I administered the first of many doses of the prescribed droplets into her mouth.

Before this, Hope would take droplets of water or ice swabs in a gentle way and slowly let the water settle down her throat, but she instinctively rejected the first dose of euthanasic liquid and let it dribble from her lips. My memory is cloudy: I'm not sure if I said anything to her, but she clearly did not want to die. In her determined-to-live mind, the mounted medical knights were still on their way to rescue her. I left the room crying profusely and didn't know what to do.

Hope was a physical vegetable in all regards; her calcium levels indicated she was supposed to have heart failure, her family was dying with her, and I was the caregiver to toil over it all. For seven long years I was the designated driver of my wife's illness—and now was the supreme test.

I gathered my tears back into my eyes and returned to the room where my wife lay. I embarked on a conversation no one ever expects to have in his or her entire life. I lay down on the bed next to Hope and hugged her deeply. I knew she could feel my embrace but couldn't respond. Her mouth reflected no emotion, only a stillness of muscle I never thought possible in a living person. I brought my lips to my wife's ear and whispered in the softest voice:

"Hope, I love you so much. I have been the luckiest man on this planet. But you have got to let go. There are no medicines or treatments left to save you. I promise you, my dear wife. We have worked as a team for seven long years, but now nothing is left. What do you want me to do? Please, with all your might, try to move your eyelids once for yes and twice for no. Please tell me what to do. Please."

Somehow Hope managed to communicate with the faintest motion of an eye. After many minutes she told me to stop all medicine. She saved me the indignity of ending her life; saved me from a hurt I would never be able to truly forgive myself for.

After this exchange of instructions, I told her, "I love you and will miss you forever."

And then one, and only one, tear eased out of her eyelid and ever so slowly ran down her soft check. I can never forget the sight of that one teardrop that foretold my entire future without her. It was a tear of regret, a tear of goodbye, a tear of wishes, a tear of never being able to embrace her best friend again, a tear of true love.

Two hours later, I held my wife's hand as her breathing slowly subsided. As her life slipped away, her angelic appearance illuminated the room. Then, as I looked upon her face, her breathing ceased and her gorgeous eyes opened and she smiled at me. She died so happy, knowing she'd a marvelous life and a lifelong best friend.

A few hours later the funeral director entered her room to remove Hope's body. She said, "I rarely see such a face as your wife's. She was one happy woman and must have loved you so much." I did not answer. I was playing the Harry Nilsson song *Without You* as they removed her.

I am learning that I'm never without Hope, and her last tear is the life force to embark on my next joyous journey. To me, that single small droplet is bigger than the universe. I live by that tear. Over the last few years it has turned from sadness into joy and from regret into a future. For me that tear is one of living life every day to its fullest. The tear has emboldened me to experience global bucket-list adventures and has reacquainted me with lust and love. The tear has directed me to reduce my psychological stress to a minimum and has enlightened me not to sweat the small stuff. The tear has taught me to trust Divinity, and most important, Hope's tear has taught me to enjoy every single day no matter if the rain is pouring or the sun is shining.

I am living and savoring the joys of life. Hope's tear is a constant reminder that when it's my turn to cry my last tear I'll be satisfied that I lived a life with no regret.

Chapter Five

Decisions

It was Hope's decision never to take birth control pills, even though statistics indicate they might lessen the chances of ovarian cancer.

It was Hope's decision never to breastfeed our children, even though statistics indicate that breastfeeding might lessen the chances of ovarian cancer.

It was Hope's decision not to have her uterus removed after she'd had numerous fibroid tumors, even though statistics indicate that surgery might lessen the chances of ovarian cancer.

It was Hope's decision, once the cancer entered her bones, not to change from the chemotherapy doctor she'd been with seven years to a venerable doctor who specialized in this form of cancer.

So why do I hate myself for not being more forceful in guiding Hope's decisions? Why can't I just live with the fact that these were her decisions and I am not responsible for them or for her death? Why?

Chapter Six

Divinity, Part One — Understanding

I THINK I'VE FELT death more than most people my age, dozens of deaths. I didn't witness their actual passing, except for Hope's, but experienced their deaths prior to their passing. Each was accompanied by the sad, disheartening, and gut-wrenching thought: *not another.* Young people, old people, and some very famous people, most in their forties or fifties. Several stand out in my memory.

The cascade began with a fifteen-year-old hockey player I coached. Tears streamed from my eyes, hidden by sunglasses, as one of the pallbearers escorting his casket down the aisle in the packed church. Afterward, at the cemetery, I'll never forget watching his father leaving the gravesite only to return and kneel as if asking his son to come back from the grave. He performed this ritual of return to the fresh-dug grave time after time, as if trying to hold on to his son. I drove away from the cemetery emotionally exhausted.

I looked into the eyes of a famous musician in his early forties, the eyes of supreme creativity. His stare was not of the music he made, but of his final goodbye. He died a few days later.

It was the same gaze I saw from little Ally, in her twenties. She was curled up in a fetal ball and glanced at me for the briefest moment. That stare, oh, that stare.

And Sharon's, the first stare I didn't recognize, and I mistook it for rudeness when really she had just found out her fight was over. Immediately after Sharon left the doctor's office I was told of her fate. I felt so ignorant and self-centered that I hated myself for days for this misunderstanding, which was reinforced when she passed several days later.

I never got to see the stare of a famous movie actress. Ann Bancroft and Hope shared the same doctor. During Hope's first major surgery, her room was directly across from Ms. Bancroft's. I hugged her husband, Mel Brooks, a famous comedian, director, and producer, minutes after she died. I'll always recall his stare and his words as he looked me in the eyes and said, "This will not be your wife's fate," and then hugged me tight like I was his son. How could the brilliance of a stare be so wrong coming from such a revered genius?

Hope was in the hospital for well over two months. A mutual friend moved into a room next to hers—not to recover but to die. Over the next week we saw less and less of her husband Rob. I slept on a cot next to Hope every night. We could feel death wait through the walls. Then one evening, at around 2:00 AM, a wail of emotion pierced our shared wall. As our friend had just passed, I jumped out of my cot and snuggled in next to Hope on her gurney. We cried with them, hugging, kissing, and cherishing each other. We couldn't see their stares, but they painted a ghostly tableau on the wall of our room.

Once you learn the eyes of death, each one is different and unique. Each person's stare is his or her personal communication of death as they try to tell you a final farewell without having to utter those terrible words. At this juncture, each person has no choice but to accept their personal choice of the Divine. I never asked anyone if they believed in Divinity at this moment, not even Hope, but with each person's passing I question Divinity for myself. I use *Divinity* deliberately rather than use the word "G-d," which is too absolute. *Divinity* permits this supreme power to remain open to question until we find out upon our own passing.

My belief in Divinity can be summed up very easily: Divinity is either omnipotence or modern physics. Divinity and science are approaching a singularity. When I die, I believe I will know which, if either, is correct, but till then it's a question without an answer. Nonetheless, I'm convinced that an energy of unparalleled force influences, interferes, and plays—sometimes gently and sometimes ferociously—in our lives. I genuinely believe that everything happens for a reason. It is for the participant to discover the reasons for each occurrence.

How does this figure into the central idea behind this book? We are about to discover, through my personal experiences, what I believe were the reasons why Hope died. The pain of life also carries the seeds of its pleasures, and I believe this concept somehow plays a role.

Chapter Seven

Hole Heart/Whole Heart

YOU ARE NOW ALONE. Single again after years with your spouse. Your Whole Heart collapses to half its size when she passes. It transfigures into what I call a Hole Heart. The Whole Heart is built upon years of shared moments—laughing and crying together over a favorite movie, sorrows at the passing of grandparents and other loved ones, feeling scared silly as we buy our first home, joy upon the birth of each child, caring for each other as we recover from any serious illness, celebrating the passing of each decade of birthdays, and the pride of marking yet another cherished anniversary together even as we watch many other couples disintegrate.

When a spouse passes, all these precious memories are dissected from your Whole Heart with a scalpel's precision, the art of forming a family and its future expunged. The years of arguments, the torment of paying bills, bickering over the cost of a vacation versus saving for retirement and squirreling away for college become wasted. Compared to the once-complacent Whole Heart, which took life for granted, the Hole Heart is deep, defining, and painfully new.

The process of resurrecting the heart to wholeness is like a Lego construction, built one deliberate brick at a time. At first, bricks of varying shapes and sizes are sorted through and meticulously placed, and slowly assume the weight and shape of the newly imagined Whole Heart.

How grueling the repair process becomes as you try to imagine what your new life will be. Just when you feel you're making strides, the blocks are torn apart, just as kindergartners at play knock down each other's creations. You sit helpless as you watch the bricks tumble, and know you must pick up the pieces. Like any kindergartner, you're frustrated yet keen to repair the damage. You long for understanding, but even kindred spirits who've also lost a loved one can't feel your individual Hole Heart. It's unique to you. Slowly, deliberately, repairs come as the pieces start to reform and the heart becomes a Whole Heart once again.

As the process unfolds, it's easy to succumb to the pleasures of aloneness. What a wonderful revelation to have to satisfy no one but yourself! Ah, to decide when and what to eat, where to vacation, what TV show or movie to watch, and how to please only oneself without interference from "another." The Hole Heart wages war within your mind, forcing you daily to choose sides, hammering at your previous understanding of the joys of marriage. The Hole Heart itself becomes the enemy as it tries to redefine happiness. The war rages on, with battles lost and won over your "need of one" or "freedom from the need of one."

And then comes the dating game, which tends to overshadow need of one in favor of freedom from need. Freedom is tempting: To date and enjoy multiple women as the inclination allows is exciting. One woman is fun at the movies, another at the museum, another on a hike in the woods, and another a passionate romp in bed. Each eventually departs in reaction to your boredom—or worse, she rejects you. You ask, "Why can't there be just one woman who can make my heart whole again?"

Each dating defeat adds to your indecision. It hurts too much to recreate the Whole Heart. It took decades to create the Whole Heart. How can another loving, nurturing, but untested and not yet trusted partner foster a process that took so long? The inner battle rages, with little compassion spared for yourself and sometimes little shown for others. Do you want the need of one or freedom from the need? Each is neither friend nor foe but an attempt to end the war.

The choice equates to the question "Do you prefer vanilla or chocolate ice cream?" Both are fine. There's no correct or incorrect choice, but devour either in excess and you sicken yourself. Choose a side without real conviction and the demolition of your new Whole Heart begins again. The Whole Heart War becomes a savage obsession.

In this conflict, innocent people become battle statistics. You lash out at friends, family, children, and dating playmates with indifference, disrespect, and even malice as you scramble to find a mental foothold to craft a vision of your future life. The tormenting cycle is repeated until you reach a final decision.

My choice is to never let my heart be satisfied without another person. I choose the need of one, and I'm fortunate that I can make that choice. Others willingly choose, with fanfare, freedom from the need from one. They no longer wish to share their lives but live as happy singles for a spell or for eternity. And there are those who are forced to accept freedom from need. They have no choice due to age or other external circumstances, and submit to the realization that they must live the life of freedom. These individuals accept that they will never have the spousal sharing of pleasures, and they learn a new way of joy, making each individual choice or acceptance for their own futures.

Whole Heart is an internal process of personal renewal. With acceptance and vision, we endeavor to make our Whole Heart again in this new life of ours. For many of us, we feel the Divine has interceded in this new future, and we actually become closer to the Divine rather than drift further away. We find a different Divinely intended creative role to contribute positively to our life and those around us.

I wish my fellow single travelers the best of luck in making their Whole Hearts. I have full Divine trust that in time my Hole Heart will be a Whole Heart, as it once was a long and short time ago.

Chapter Eight

The Awakening, Part One — Serpent Tongue

DO YOU REMEMBER YOUR first kiss? Were you twelve, fourteen? Younger? Older? The age doesn't matter, but the anticipation in tingling lip sensation does. I was in ninth grade, and I don't even remember her name. I was shy and totally out of my element. Having just graduated from neighborhood youth games to a first date was monumental for a street hound of the 1960s. At my current age, all I remember of that first kiss is that it was in a movie theater and was luscious. She had on teenage cherry lip-gloss that made the taste hang on my lips. It was like slowly licking a cherry lollipop. We never went on the second date, I don't remember why, but to this day I remember that delicious cherry taste.

In thirty-two years I kissed only one woman, other than Hope, on the lips. It was a short goodbye kiss with no pretense of romance. It was a temptation of another life maybe, knowing that the time in this life wasn't right. It was about twelve years before Hope passed, when our marriage was faltering, but somehow I knew we would make it right, so the kiss was more a goodbye than an opening. For thirty-two years my mouth knew only one pair of lips, Hope's, sometimes with just a peck and sometimes a long, lovemaking kiss. Either way, every single morning and evening for thirty-two years, on awakening, coming home from work, and going to bed at night, I was either greeted or put to sleep with the same tried-and-true lips. Oh, boy, they were so comforting and familiar. I took the simple acts of daily pleasure for granted. The universe says they're gone forever.

Was it the familiarity or just knowing they were always there and mine alone that made me think those lips would remain mine forever? I don't think Hope ever kissed anyone else either, and that she was true to me. During our turbulent years, I always thought she might have had a fling, but all the housecleaning of history after her death never revealed any indication of any unfaithfulness. I think, like me, Hope had visions and fantasies, but was too afraid to risk losing our family and the hard work of cooperation we'd built over decades. As I write this, I feel comfortable that had I died first, her first new kiss in thirty-two years would have been just like mine—a romantic comedy.

I didn't practice my kissing for the first new lips to touch. Who would have thought to practice? After all, doesn't thirty-two years make you an expert? Doesn't experience count? Wow, what an innocent fool!

Fortyish and attractive, she had medium-length, straight blond hair and was just a tad overweight, as are most of us who try hard to look good but still love to eat. I would say she was soft like a teddy bear. I don't remember the peripherals, but the kiss itself is a highlight of memory, as is my first kiss in ninth grade. I'll spare you the details of the prelude to embrace. It was actually quite boring, but I'll jolly you with the actual kiss. I had no preparation for the coming mind-flummox.

My companion was a divorcee of many years and a knowledgeable kisser, or so I thought. We started to kiss normally and passionately, and then she suddenly rammed her tongue into my mouth. It wasn't French-kissing tenderness, but more like a serpent on the hunt, its spear-like tongue searching for its prey and, having found it, going in for the kill. My mind went awash, frantically trying to figure out what the heck was going on as I struggled at a supposedly enjoyable activity I had performed with no problems for thirty-two years. Her tongue was searching deep in my mouth for a response, I mean full-tongue deep! I pulled away and like an embarrassed novice asked, "Sorry, what are you doing?"

Now I've learned some lessons from dating a plethora of women: Some are sensitive and some insensitive. They don't necessarily mean their quick answers; it's just them. Her answer, actually how she shared it, made me feel like an incompetent bonehead. It was similar to the first time in class you eagerly, with impatience, raise your hand to answer a teacher's question and the insensitive, hard-ass teacher dismisses the answer with condescending indifference, demonstrating to the class what a fool you are. You learn quickly never to volunteer unless chosen. It is the same with dating and the mistakes of dating.

Back to the kiss: my date's response was not reassuring.

"What, you never kissed like this? This is how it is done where I grew up." She repeated it again to inflict her point. "You never kissed like this? I have done this always."

Well, maybe I was oversensitive and took her response as a jab at my manly prowess. Or maybe she was just condescending. It really didn't matter. What mattered was I just realized I wasn't prepared for this new single dating life. I was a novice, a fourteen-year-old at fifty-four stumbling at the dating scene all over again. It wasn't pretty the first time, and now, with remembered battle scars still secreted in the folds of my brain, it wasn't pretty again.

After the few seconds of realization, I became the student for whom many women love to take the position of teacher. My date explained to me that one person sticks a tongue deep in the other's mouth while the receiving person sucks on the tongue as it is slowly pulled out. Then the process is repeated and shared. The routine, or should I say kissing fun, goes from normal kissing to serpent-devil tongue kissing by both partners, and back to normal kissing. This process is repeated until boredom sets in or you jump into the sack for more mistakes—for this wasn't my only mistake that evening, but the only one I dare share if I'm to salvage any self-respect.

You see, the mistakes for a widower don't begin or end with the kiss. A man must perform. I'll save those tears of laughter and self-deprecation for another chapter. Back again to the kiss: I'm an engineer, and my nature is to execute all tasks and responsibilities correctly. I remembered reading *Men's Health* magazine in a doctor's office. (If you don't know, it's the *Cosmo* for men.) After that first kiss, I decided I was going to learn to become the Don Juan of kissing. I wanted to be a man who knew how to kiss passionately and make love with sensuous caring while savoring each new romantic interlude as I explored a new heavenly body. For thirty-two years, complacency had made me comfortable, but I discovered each woman had a different notion of kissing and intimacy. Each one was a whole new learning experience. I learned, as a man who wanted to bring pleasure, that the woman was always right, and I, the man, was always wrong. It didn't matter if they had a serpent for a tongue or no tongue at all. I wanted to please them, and it was up to me to find their reality. In fact, I kissed more than seventy-five women, and no other woman knew of serpent tongue, as I called it. I tried the serpent-tongue technique on a few other women, and each withdrew in bewildered disgust.

I had learned the lesson: Each woman is unique. I wanted to be prepared for every experience and therefore studied *Men's Health* and other publications to please the women who welcomed and trusted me. Occasionally, I made really stupid and inconsiderate mistakes, for which I sincerely apologize to every one of those women I fumbled on. I was a good man and husband for thirty-two years, but I was making hurtful intimacy mistakes like a teenager. I was and am truly sorry for the feelings I hurt, but with each failure there were also successes that made the whole experience well worth it. With each success I felt closer to what was intended for my next journey.

There is a happy ending to this chapter. One woman didn't really appreciate me much on our first date, but when I kissed her goodbye as she waited to go into the taxi, some spark flew in her brain and she needed to know more. She tells me that my kiss was why she came back for a second date. I had practiced and learned through trial and error for the time it counted the most.

Chapter Nine

The Awakening, Part Two — Nair Nipples

MY BEST FRIEND, BRUCE, and I shared many intimacies, helping each other navigate the longevity of our marriages. Through the years we would spend one or more weekends a year tinkering at home, followed by evening cigars and plenty of drinks. The nights were filled with revelations about each other as the liquor pours progressed. One of my discoveries was learning that Bruce had started shaving his private parts, in his words, "so they were smooth, with no hair on my balls or penis."

The thought of doing that to myself filled me with terror. Thinking aloud, I said, "First I've got to find the correct razor, or razors, then learn how to not cut my manliness."

"No, no, no," Bruce said. "Use a beard trimmer with a plastic guard—the razor is too dangerous!"

Each act of shaving became a new learning experience, and the terror never quite abated. I learned, however, that the rewards, which included a little more intimacy and the rediscovery of forgotten sex acts, were well worth the monthly dread of trimming my private parts.

Hope found this new grooming pleasing and reawakening. She once tried to get me to shave the hair off my back; that episode was a scene straight from a movie—never to be repeated. This plus the normal clipping of nose, eyebrows, and ear hair were all I had to do to please my wife. Then came John....

Several months after Hope's passing, my friend Scotty invited me to join him and his single friends on the beach. I hadn't been to the beach as a single man in thirty-two years. I loaded up my backpack, filled my Nalgene water bottle, and packed my sunscreen, a slightly worn beach towel, Native American flute, and other necessities. I bought a brand-new beach chair since Hope and I hadn't sat on the beach in more than seven years (sun and chemo didn't mix). Wearing my favorite red, non-classic bathing suit, a newly purchased stylish T-shirt, and an Oceanside Ice Hockey cap, I was ready and looking cool. Oh, did I mention my black flip-flop sandals?

It was late spring, a picture-postcard Long Island beach day with a cloudless blue sky. The sun shone bright, the kind of sun we long for all winter. There was absolutely no humidity and the air was crisp and clean. The ocean was calm, but with just enough wave break to add harmonious sound, which welcomed easy bathing without fighting the waves. It was a perfect day for me to enter a new life and adventure.

Searching the beach, I found Scotty and his crew of single friends who were in their forties and fifties. Real Long Island Irish, German, Jewish, and Italian guys who sported neatly trimmed or slicked-back hair. They were all much taller than my five-foot-five-inch stature and were almost all in good shape. What struck me was that none had any body hair and everyone was already tanned so early in the season.

Scotty introduced me to his buddies like I was the newest member of the beach gang. They welcomed me warmly, and let me know that if I was interested, I could join in the nightly bar scene too. These guys looked like men on the prowl, and they wanted the fun women. I got situated with my chair and towel, and then took off my T-shirt. I was well on the way to losing all the caregiver-anxiety weight I'd gained over the past few years, but I still had a good five pounds to lose. I wasn't by any means fat, but wasn't buff like these single guys.

After my shirt came off, one guy, John, stared at me with a shocked, disapproving expression. It wasn't my weight that startled him, but my "look"—the look of long ape-like hair on my body and under-arms, and basically all of my hair everywhere. Like a companion I'd known for years, even though it was only ten minutes, John called me aside from the pack of unattached prowlers. He had advice to share. He wanted me to be gang-worthy.

"Hey, Den," he said. "You need to groom that mess and look neat. You got to be at your best for the one who'll count—you know, the one you really want."

And then John kindly and sympathetically proceeded to instruct me on how a single man should groom himself to avoid turning off the ladies. After his detailed re-imaging, he advised me on how to remove my unwanted hair by waxing my body or using even quicker and cheaper ways, such as applying the hair remover Nair.

"Nair?" I said. "Like the TV commercials for women?"

John answered yes, but revealed that they made extra-strength Nair for removing tough, manlike hair. Intrigued, I actually thought it quite amusing to try. Remembering the past waxing experience of my hair, Nair seemed like an easy, no-fear substitute for unforgotten pain. The conversation concluded with the usual etiquette that ends a conversation when the teacher has nothing more to impart. I must have made a good impression because the guys invited me out to the local Friday night singles scene when beach day ended. I was part of the gang!

A typical guy who wants action and to be loved again, I went from the beach to the local drugstore to buy some Nair. This was the second time since Hope died that I entered a drugstore to buy items I hadn't purchased in decades. Some weeks before, prior to a date, I had bought some condoms. (I don't want to leave you hanging, so yes, I got to use them.) What an experience to buy condoms after twenty-odd years. Who knew there were dozens of different kinds: colors, scents, lubrication, ribbed, reservoir end, shaped and sized for big and small penises?

As I looked for condoms, my friend Chris called me on my cell to see how I was doing. He often checked in on me. I love that sweet-hearted man for his true, rare, unselfish caring. He was one of the few people who really helped me through the years with a very welcome "You all right?" phone call. Anyway, Chris had a crisp sense of humor. As I searched among the condoms, he said, "Why don't you buy one of those types for the really huge penis. When you go to bed with a woman, take the package out with the lights on. Then turn off the lights and switch to a condom really meant for guys like us." My male ego answered, "I really need the big one," and laughed with him. Chris always knew how to make me feel good—even in such an awkward moment.

I found the Nair by myself, embarrassed to ask any of the employees where it was. There were several types of hair removers and brands with different applicators. As an "engineering project," I read every label and reread several until, after about forty-five minutes, I selected three types with different applicators. One was a cream with a sponge applicator, another a cream with a scraper, and the third a spray for hard-to-reach areas in the back. I even bought a long-handled shower brush to help me in the tough-to-reach places. If I was going to do this I was going to do it right and get every bit of gorilla hair the first time around.

I also made a stop at the condom aisle. Maybe I'd get lucky tonight, and a new type of condom would be fun. For the record I went home that night dejected and depressed. I had entered the Long Island bar scene I'd so despised thirty-two years before. Hating my life, I cried myself to sleep. Boy, was I lucky to have found find my mate when I was twenty-one, escaping that horrific single life I so dreaded. Unfortunately, I was learning again that the single life, at least for me, was a crock of shit and lies created by magazines. It's mostly a life of sadness and loneliness punctuated with taunting glimpses of fantasies becoming reality for a few hours, only to leave you drained of all emotion and energy.

I left the drugstore and went home curious to fashion a new Dennis. I stripped and went into the bathroom to start the new ritual. First, I gazed at my body in the mirror with an altered awareness. *Wow,* I thought, *I do look like an ape.* I planned meticulously, like an engineer, how I'd use the different types of applicators and products to remove the hair on my chest and back.

I unwrapped the heavy-duty hair remover, breaking the plastic with my teeth, and read the instructions about as carefully as someone rushing to get on with it. With bottle and sponge applicator in hand I entered the shower, squirted the paste-like white lotion on the sponge, and applied thick layers of the stuff to my chest.

Hey, this is easy, I thought.

I let the cream sit for the prescribed seconds and then used a curved plastic scraper to remove the hair. Clumps of it, in random Mondrian-like patterns, fell off my chest, leaving some areas as bare as a baby's behind and others with more hair. My chest resembled a checkerboard—a checkerboard of a disappearing old me.

I decided to use the extra-strong cream first, and then do a second pass with another lotion. I also began to wonder how I was going to remove the hair from my back. After a few seconds' deliberation, I embraced the long scrub brush and moved in front of the huge mirror over the sink. In contorted strokes, I placed the stuff over half my back, ever so aware of the product label, which warned not to keep the lotion on my body longer than the prescribed time. I had nightmare visions of toxic ooze and my skin coming off in sheets. I entered the shower again to brush away the cream.

Have you ever tried to just wash your back with one of those brushes? The effort is frustrating. Now try to imagine scrubbing to remove decades of hair. I gained some muscle that day in places

I'd never had to work out before. Soon, most of my upper body hair was gone.

On to the finishing touches: I used the spray to remove the last lingering hairs on my torso and then decided to venture down to my privates. Despite the warning on the bottle not to spray the testicles, I said "What the hell. How bad can it be?" and applied some to my testicles. Oh, my God! Instantly, I felt like my balls were locked in a vise that was crushing them like a rubber ball being compressed into a marble. I grabbed the hand-held showerhead and rushed water over my scrotum for what seemed an eternity, until the frightful squeezing sensation abated. Woo, never again!

With that excruciating ordeal over, I applied the spray to areas that still had hair—like my nipples. Another major mistake that made me wince in agony. Both nipples pulsated and stung. I once again tried to extinguish my error with the shower spray until the pain subsided. Little did I know that the pain would last for weeks: My nipples became so sore that the slightest rubbing against a shirt felt like sandpaper. For weeks I tried different salves, creams, and other remedies to lessen the pain. At night, I slept with Band-Aids on my nipples. On weekends, I was at the mercy of whatever activity I was doing. I had to either endure the pain or risk bleeding through my shirt.

The pain eventually subsided, but my hair grew back coarse and prickly. My curly ape-like hair, soft from years of growth, had become cactus needles! Once again I took to the shower and applied hair remover. This time it was a quick job because so little hair had to go. This became a ritual for an entire summer. I don't think I ever wished beach days to be over so quickly. The Nair procedure was becoming tiresome, and worse, I began to wonder what lasting chemical effects there might be on my body and internal organs. After that experimental summer I decided that if a woman wanted me she would need to love me for me, ape-like hair and all. I was not going to repeat this, just as I had told Hope many years before that I'd never wax my back again. The pain was just too great.

I was still single, but was learning how to be single on my own terms—a difficult task for a man who'd shared every bit of his life for thirty-two years with one woman, a woman who'd laugh at his mistakes and guide him in his quests. Many a night I asked Hope for guidance, even thought she was no longer in worldly physical presence. Hope's counsel came to me as I asked the Divine. The underlining message was to be myself and trust all that had occurred over the past decade.

Hope wasn't with me any longer on this earth, but with her Divine guidance, my explorations and discoveries continued with abandon.

Chapter Ten

A Hundred Bottles of Beer on the Wall

WHEN I WAS A Cub Scout in the 1960s we sometimes took very long bus trips—at least they seemed long for boys who experienced most of their travels on Schwinn bikes. On these monotonous bus trips we sang the youthful ancient mariner songs to make the miles pass faster. One of our favorites was *100 Bottles of Beer on the Wall*. We started enthusiastically, the entire Cub pack, strong voiced and full of confidence. As the bottles fell off the wall one by one, the strength of our song diminished, and one bored scout after another dropped out. There were always one or two youngsters who kept going until a fellow scout, aggressively interrupted the still-singing stragglers with a new tune, and the repetitive youthful bravado began again to a song such as "Walking down Canal Street knocking on every door. I will be a son of a bitch if I can find a whore. Finally found..."

For me, finding a new soul mate was like counting those beers falling off the wall. So many times I wanted to quit singing and not go on. Maybe I was always the last one still singing before a new song arrived.

After my wife died, my coworker and friend, Richie, and I would hang out and dream about our futures. I was a widower and he a recent divorcee. After each date I went on, and shared with him, he would say, "Dude, you expect too much." I would explain to Richie that if I was going to do this again, I would want it all or nothing—always emphasizing the selfish word "want." "Dude," I said, "I'm not settling. I want an adventurous woman who will scuba dive, hike glaciers to deserts, and travel to remote places, an accomplished skier who loves to enjoy the outdoors. I want a woman who's passionate and loves sex as much as I do and who doesn't make me feel "dirty" when I want a raw quickie, innovative, or timeless sex. So many of my dates placed outcomes or requirements with each sex act. I want a woman who's a good mother and whose children are nice. I want a woman who's accomplished in a career. I want an opinionated woman who'll give me "shit" back. I want a woman who will open new doors to topics I don't know anything about. I want a partner who'll grow with me, love me for who I am, and look at life through the same lens as I do.

"Okay, Dennis, have fun searching," Richie would say, his tone implying that my expectations weren't realistic.

Search isn't the proper word to use in my pursuit of a new partner. I think "career" is more apt. My cousin Craig and I were going through simultaneous life changes. Recently divorced, Craig observed that I took on the task of finding a new partner the same way I performed my job. I'm a construction engineer, expediter, manager, and creator. I used every ounce of thirty-five years' professional management experience to make my search for a new life mate successful, and yes, I took this on as a job that I'd pursue devotedly till the love drug filled my veins again.

I'd had a truly fantastic marriage with Hope. Like a habit-forming drug, I missed it and longed for it. I was going through the heebie-jeebies of withdrawal. I needed the companionship drug to fulfill my mind and soul.

My dating escapades were the target of jokes from friends and family. I became their entertainment. My sons, in judgment and non-acceptance, either ignored or frowned upon my endeavors and my "new friends."

Let's examine the things I did—perceived as ridiculous—to score the love drug. I used bullet points to keep track, just as I would at work to manage a project. After all it was my new career!

♦ *Dating Websites*

- Engage in two to four dating websites at any one time: Match.Com, JDate, Adventure Singles, Widow.com and others.

- When truly desperate for a woman with shared fantasies of intimacy, I explored Ashley Madison* and Seeking Arrangements. I tried Tinder, but I guess my matches never ignited anyone.

♦ *Profiles, Interests, Likes, Dislikes*

I wrote one profile after another trying to score the perfect match or sex partner depending on which site I was using. Friends and relatives offered expert suggestions except on "alternative" websites that I kept secret. I often wonder how they would have written those bios.

♦ *No responses.*

- What am I doing wrong?

- I'm a great guy.

- Too forward.

---

*   Ashley Madison was recently hacked. I received an email that if I didn't pay a specified website the information would be released to my friends, wife, and the entire world. I laughed with glee knowing my book would do the same for free!

- Not forward enough.

- Do I seem like a jerk?

- Am I too short? Should I lie about my height? No, I hate women who lie to me and run fast from them for the slightest infraction or perception of lying.

Taking pictures became a passion as the seasons changed, I lost weight, I sorted specific responses, posted to websites, etc. Beach scenes, dress shirts, no shirt, shorts, casual, formal, skiing, hiking, with my children, etc. I tried them all. A number of women said I looked much better in person. One said, "You're very cute, not like your picture."

How do I portray my cuteness? I deemed I wasn't photogenic, and if I didn't find Ms. Right soon I'd need a professional photographer to make me look like the real me.

As for photography, many women used false photos of themselves. Several stand out most.

I traveled one hour to meet this dream girl. Everything on her profile beamed Ms. Right, but when I met her it turned out she was much older than her picture, which was taken over ten years prior. What was she thinking? Or was she desperate, like so many of us, unhappy to be alone?

Another was a woman on one of the "alternative sites." A beautiful photo adorned her page. When I met her she was many—I mean *many*—pounds heavier. I had never dated a woman much heavier than I. She turned out to be delightful and we had a fun evening as I erased a misguided prejudice.

Another woman posted a picture that was so cute and suburban, just like a woman I could hug in a movie theater for a lifetime. When we met, my eyes bulged out of their sockets in disbelief, like a cartoon character. Then I uttered, "You don't look anything like your picture."

She was deeply hurt. I found a way to recover and apologize. We actually sat down and had dinner for an hour. It turned out she'd had her photo digitally "enhanced." She also ran website seminars. I guess I was one of her test subjects.

- Write cooing first emails to entice the bird of the other sex to respond.

- How many other birds did I have to fight off for that "beauty" in the photo?

- Did I get there first?

- Why don't they like me?

- Please, I want to meet you.

- Spending countless hours trying to sort through the hundreds of profiles and emails.

- Two to three dates, meetings, interviews… a week from the websites, bars, causal meetings, blind dates, etc.

- Where do we meet?

- Too far to travel? Limit distances by profile.

- Bar and scene hopping one to two nights a week when not dating.

Weekends out to 5:00 AM with no curfew, acting just like a drunken college kid. Yes, we still get the "icks"* at fifty-three years of age after an inebriated experience we wish not to remember.

I could add much more to this list, but I'll spare you the boredom. My kids thought I'd lost it. Their dad was a teenager and they were

---

*   "Icks" is slang for disgust. Growing up, we used it for disgust for oneself or another, a date, or even food.

my parents. Each month I tormented them with a new "She's the one and I'm in love." They laughed at me and with me, and lambasted me as close friends do. Like parents, they refrained from giving advice except at the junctures when it was most needed. We forged a new understanding of our relationship during this period. They were no longer my children but my equals and dear friends as we exchanged sound advice.

I had met some wonderful women in this process. One stands out. She was kind, considerate, intelligent, and fun, but after a few months I knew it wasn't right. She gave me this insight to keep on searching: "You must date over a hundred women to find the one," she said. She too was on a quest and was not giving up. The rabbi I met in the hospital, and to whom I dedicated this book, was correct in saying that every meeting had a purpose. That wise woman ended up marrying one of my friends. As for me, I kept on singing *One Hundred Bottles of Beer* ....

Almost every date, short-term relationship, bar scene, one-night stand, or "alternate" experience ended with heartbreak. Wishing I was dead, feelings of utter emptiness, hatred of the world—why me, what did I do to deserve this? I'm ugly, I am mean and a terrible person, I'm too nice, I should give up and just live alone for the remainder of my life—pervaded my soul.

If not for Betty Hill Crowson—our counselor since the beginning of Hope's illness—and the Divine, I think I might have committed suicide. So many times I just wanted to end the misery and dreamt of putting a shotgun to my mouth as Kurt Cobain had done. I would play Nirvana's unplugged album, especially the song *Man Who Sold the World* as my dreams alternated between death and future hope. Oh, the inner torment that drives such selfish fantasies that would impart an even deeper hurt to my children, already aching from their mom's recent passing.

I wanted—no, needed—that drug of companionship, trusted friendship, and deep love. My dealer was nowhere to be found, I was in withdrawal, and was doing cruel, stupid things. I was destroying myself and everyone around me, as addicts inflict pain on those near to them. Twice I had to swear off alcohol for the disgusting things it caused me to say and do. I apologized to everyone I hurt and wronged when I was drunk and stupid or just plain sober and even more stupid.

I thank the Divine for being there or this book would not have been written. Instead my ashes would have been scattered around the lake as Hope's were. Often I wanted my ashes to mingle in the copper-tinted waters of Otis Reservoir, the lake my home overlooks in Massachusetts, so my addiction could be satisfied in a different way. I couldn't find peace in this way of life, and death was a form of peace I contemplated. Just as my Hole Heart was resigned to always being Hole, my friend decided I had earned a reprieve.

What reprieve? It haunts me still. When Hope's death was certain, I was with some friends a few weeks before she passed. I boasted that after Hope's death I would be free to live again and to experiment with women. I felt I had been denied years of pleasure during her illness and had earned my right to experiment after three decades of marriage. The Divine, after Hope's death, gave me what I wished for that night in women—tall, short, skinny, fat, young, older, Asian, Black, Hispanic, Indian, blond, brunette, etc. Like all the genie-in-the-bottle jokes, be careful of your last wish, for it may be misconstrued.

My friend watched me with utter glee as one watches a cut worm writhe, trying to make it onto the grass before the sun dries the body, to grow whole again. Isn't it truly amazing how a worm can grow whole from half a body? I found out we mortals can too.

Chapter Eleven

Ego Penis

A MAN'S EGO CENTERS on his thoughts about his penis, thus the phrase "Ego Penis." From the time boys begin to talk about their penises till the day they die, the penis remains one of the most important topics. It arises everywhere—street youth banter and hideout discussions, high school locker rooms, male bonding sessions, conference-room jokes, etc. From an early age, we learn the nonsense that size matters, which we casually dismiss with phrases like "It's not the boat but the motion" to ease our feelings of perceived genital inadequacy.

When our penis works perfectly, we're at peace with our sexuality and can deal with all of life's other complications. Issues of size, frequency, or too-quick ejaculation don't plague us. When our penis doesn't work to our liking, we're distracted at work and in love. Penile insecurities invade our mind's well-being. A simple conversation that includes the penis issue often elicits dark thoughts about our performance or lack of it, so we're distracted from happiness until we can let go of our Ego Penis and think about other things instead.

As a long-time married man I knew from experience that penis function ebbs and flows over time. There are times when we feel like Hercules and times when we feel like Elmer Fudd. Women too have their sexual insecurities. Over time, the ebbs and flows of marriage and intimate companionship impact sexual desire and performance for both spouses. We learn to assist, compliment, fix, and be patient with each other's mismatched—or absent—sexuality. Marital friction, cheating, and divorce may occur when one partner lacks humility or an understanding of the other's sexual needs.

Caregivers like me face special challenges. The length of a loved one's illness erodes a caregiver's Ego Penis and positive mental outlook. When a spouse is gravely ill there is simply no intimacy or even the thought of intimacy. In time a male caregiver's ability to perform erodes to the point where he can't get an erection while masturbating or even with a drug like Viagra. His sexuality is locked in a box, only to emerge when his spouse gets better or dies. His ego is in turmoil because he's no longer the man he once was, and doesn't know if he ever will be again. It is a putrid, self-deprecating feeling when he masturbates to a photo of a beautiful woman, only to give up and then switch to a violent movie to satisfy the other ego.

At this point, he wonders if another woman would change the course of events. Contemplation of cheating enters into a life once committed to monogamy. As the caregiver's sexuality is eventually destroyed, the primeval sexual instinct tears at his moral compass. This experience may differ from that of a person who's in the military or working far from home. That person can go home to a healthy spouse; the caregiver doesn't know if his beloved's health will ever return.

I remember two occasions when I felt tempted to cheat while Hope was in the hospital. I hadn't had intercourse for many months. My only sexual pleasure was masturbation when my penis permitted. In the hospital, I had met two women who were in similar predicaments. They too were long-term caregivers to stage IV cancer patients. We spent many weeks together as our spouses tried to hang on to life. Both women's husbands eventually died of cancer during their hospital stays.

We felt strong sexual energies and tensions when we interacted with each other. I think if we'd met in a private area, we would have ripped each other's clothes off just to feel a naked body next to ours. For many reasons, including my fear of sexual non-performance, the fantasized encounter never happened, for my ego and my penis were now ruined. I had forgotten how to please a woman, or feared that I no longer could. I was worried about being impotent or ejaculating too soon. A woman can, if she wishes, lie there and pretend, but a man needs to perform. If there's no Viagra available, oh, no! If he ejaculates within seconds, yikes!

Eventually Hope passed away, and for a while my sexuality died with her. I was bloated and fat; most of the time I couldn't get an erection even with medication, and if I did get erect, I ejaculated in seconds or minutes. I felt I had nothing to offer women.

After Hope passed and I was told that her childhood best friend had stage IV cancer. I decided to change and start to live again. I wanted to feel joy again, and I wanted sex again. I wanted "Penthouse Letters" sex. I wanted X-rated movie sex. I wanted uncommitted sex. I wanted committed sex. I wanted it all and felt it was due me, but I knew I had to work at it.

I went to a urologist who specialized in improving male sexuality. He was in his sixties, and was extremely compassionate. As I told him my story I broke down in hysterical tears. I could see his eyes water too as my story unfolded. Calmly, gently, he explained that male impotency and duration of performance were common among widowers. He told me to be compassionate to myself and to accept myself for who I am. Over time my sexuality would return, he explained, but only if my mind led the way. The condition wasn't physical, he said, but existed entirely in my head. To feel better, I had to begin repairing my mind and ego as much as I focused on improving my body.

And so the healing process began. I commenced a daily exercise regime to tone my body and shed pounds quickly. I wanted to live positively, and explored various avenues through classes at the Kripalu Center for Yoga and Health in Massachusetts, the Open

Center in New York City, and through self-help books. I embraced Toltec wisdom through the writings and lectures of Don Miguel Ruiz and Sheri Rosenthal. I read *Men's Health* magazine and everything I could find to reacquaint myself with becoming a skilled and compassionate lover. I talked to friends about how to become a sexual being again, and, several months after Hope's death, I began dating. Many people condemned me for this, but I concluded that if I stayed on the path I was on I'd be unable to recover from my abyssal grief.

As I reacquainted myself with dating and sex, some women understood my awkwardness, some made me feel inadequate, and with some I performed pretty well except for one major issue: I could no longer ejaculate while having sex. It felt like I was ejaculating, but nothing came out. As I wore condoms most of the time, the women didn't know of my problem. In fact, I faked an orgasm many times. (Yes, men can do that too!). I was using Cialis, and my penis would remain hard for as long as I wanted, but I would only complete sex after I faked ejaculation.

With one woman I didn't wear a condom, and she made me feel terrible because of my ejaculation problem. Looking back, I think her reaction was less about me than about her frustration at feeling unable to please me. We dated for several months. She made me feel worse and worse after each failed sexual encounter. I don't know why I kept going back for more. Maybe I felt I deserved the abuse. Eventually we let each other go. I'll share one funny story about her. To protect her privacy I'll call her Debbie, which wasn't her real name.

Debbie was a beautiful woman in her late forties. We had several mutual acquaintances. At a holiday party, I told one of our mutual acquaintances that I was dating her. We were both feeling good from the abundant alcohol, and his reply was comical: "You're dating Debbie? She's beautiful. What a body, it's perfect. Are you screwing her? You lucky man! I've dreamt of her while having sex.

What's it like? Please tell me. Is it as great as I imagine?"

To protect my own ego and hers, I never revealed that our lovemaking wasn't synchronous and was mired in complexities. I kept our lovemaking private. I did share that Debbie's body was magnificent.

I went back to the urologist and explained the situation. I was now having sex, could get an erection and last for a spell, but couldn't ejaculate. He explained the medical terminology; my condition was a form of "retrograde ejaculation." Again it was my mind, not my body. "Don't put so much pressure on yourself," he said. *Please remember these words as you read this book.* He said it would pass as I became more comfortable having sex again.

At this point in life I wanted to experiment, but to experiment well one must be in good shape for sex. Just as one trains for a sports competition, one needs to prepare for sexual activity. When you think about it, isn't sex really a sport? It requires all the preparations and offers all the rewards of a sport—endurance, confidence, skill, creativity, and achievement.

To train, I found a "house of women" willing to help me regain my sexuality and ego after Hope had passed away. I refuse to degrade these women and call them prostitutes, for they were compassionate—and also trying to make a living. They lived in suburban or urban communities with families, and could be the next-door neighbors you greeted warmly every day.

I opened myself up to these kind women. We had deep conversations about male and female sexuality and needs. We talked about their boyfriends, our dating experiences, and our future goals. They talked about their lives as I discussed mine. Each had a unique experience to share. They were like dear friends who truly cared to get me better. They made me feel comfortable over the many months I visited them. They helped me become a good lover by explaining what made them feel good, which was mostly not about the sex act but about making them feel needed, loved, and attractive. They made me feel whole again.

Also, they explained that a good majority of their clients don't have sex with them, or at least want sex only a fraction of the time. Most of the time is spent in conversation. The men just need someone to talk to and confide in.

As I had sex more often, I began to ejaculate again. These women helped renew my life, and with it my sexuality. I am forever grateful to them.

Following my experiences with these ladies, I started to enjoy sex again. There were still problems, however. I remained somewhat self-conscious and performance anxiety still pervaded every session of lovemaking with the women I dated. This began to change when I met a very special woman. During our first lovemaking session my head fell off the pillow and lay directly on the bed. She was very kind, and gently placed the pillow back under my head. I ejaculated during that first encounter, which was still a rarity with women I dated. As we lay in bed we shared deep thoughts. I told her about my sexual troubles, and she said to me, "No pressure, be yourself." The second time we made love it was outdoors and I had trouble with my erection. Again she said, "No pressure, be yourself." She made me feel relaxed and comfortable, and over the next few weeks my sexuality recovered with a teenage frenzy. My Ego Penis was back!

Chapter Twelve

Home

WE TAKE HOME FOR granted. As the metaphor says, "Home is where we hang our hat." But what is a true home to a widower after his wife has passed? Home was a place of experiences. I bought my home at the age of twenty-four, and within the first year I was married. I lived there over thirty years and never moved until a year after Hope died and our children had flown the coop. I could tell you the fairy tale of home; instead I've decided to lose the breadcrumbs and "fall off the wall."

Home is where you play ice hockey on a Friday night in lieu of cuddling with Hope in bed.

Home is where you gain weight with Hope's pregnancy but decided not to lose the extra weight as your Hope did. It's too much fun, after all, to eat more and exercise less. You know Hope will still love you the way you are.

Home is where you fought over Hope's buying that new designer handbag. How cute Hope looked with it, but out of spite you never paid her a compliment.

Home is where you played computer games until 1:00 AM. Hope pounded the floor for you to come up, but you didn't listen. She waited for you in bed only to fall asleep alone.

Home is where you had to work late even though you'd promised to be home on time. Hope waited for you as dinner got cold. Did you need to stay at work? Why did you really stay? Hope and the employer are now gone. You became disillusioned with life and work as you tried to grasp why you hadn't come home that night and so many other nights.

Home is where, for years, you squirreled away money for retirement, and just as your last child graduates from college Hope dies. She doesn't get to enjoy all the years of tough decisions and the arguments that went with them. You get to play and live your hard-earned fantasies and Hope does not.

Home is where we are in separate rooms. Hope is watching a comedy and I'm watching a violent movie. How I wish I could laugh with her one more time.

Home is where you take a walk after dinner. Hope is walking slowly, savoring the night, and you're walking fast with the patience of a two-year-old because life or TV is on your mind, not the sheer joy of having Hope by your side.

Home is where Hope is exercising on Saturdays and I'm watching or coaching the kids in sports. Who was right? Did our kids become superstars? My parents never attended my sporting events, and I don't love them any less. How I miss the days when Hope was my assistant coach in intramural ice hockey and it was a family event.

Home is where you curse out Hope in an argument and the next day regret your stinging words. Hope is gone, but the words still haunt your memory.

Home is where you don't tell Hope every day how beautiful she is.

Home is where you refuse to go shopping with Hope for new clothes. You hate clothes shopping, but it would have made her feel so good if you'd joined her and watched her try on each new outfit.

Home is where you complain constantly as you perform "honey-do" chores. You always completed them, but you could have accomplished them with a smile and not a frown.

Home is where you're out with the guys and don't bother to call Hope to tell her you'll be hours late.

Home is where you bring work home with you and don't give your family the attention they so deserve. Tragically, only as Hope's years are coming to an end do you discover how to switch off this savage circuit breaker of work.

Home is where you hold the grudge of a disagreement for days when those lost hours are never regained but the disagreement melted into the fabric of time. We learnt how a fifteen-minute "time out" solves disagreements too late in our marriage to regain those hours or days lost to needless acrimony.

Home is where Hope and I used to giggle and laugh as young lovers building a life and home together. Laughter faded as the children turned into teens and my career and fatherly demands grew. Hope laughed alone for a while, until I realized what closeness I had squandered. I regained my fun self again in the last years of Hope's life. A few years too late as my anguish over lost time never ceases.

Home is the thousands of other things I haven't mentioned that are either too mundane or trivial to you, dear reader, but ever so precious to me because I'll never have the chance to correct them. Oh, how I cry over each and every one of them as the regretful memories return.

Home is where I am a broken man from work and caring for a very sick person for seven long years. The last two months of Hope and home were not memorable—they were a rush to the end for me, and for Hope a clinging to the last vestiges of life. The doctors, social workers, and hospice nurses tell me I earned the "Gold Medal" for caregivers, but my inner self taunts me that it could have ended more peacefully for us.

And then one day you go home and the home is empty of your best friend, the person you took for granted. You wish you had lost the weight, watched the comedy with her, worked out with her, walked slowly with her, shopped with her—but it's too late for that now. Hope is never coming home again. I wrote my letter of apology to Hope and burnt it as the sage advised. As long as I believe in the Divine, Hope has received my penance. When and if I find a new home, I promise I'll try not to make those mistakes again. I promise.

Chapter Thirteen

Fucked Up

WE ARE ALL FUCKED up in one way or another. All of us. We appeal to one person and disgust another. Our mannerisms attract one and repel another. Our smell is lilacs to one and vinegar to another. With one person, sex is never-ending lust, and with another a total turnoff ("can't get it up" in man-speak). Didn't you ever think or share with a friend, "I can't figure it out. What does she see in him?"

The real hard work begins after you find someone who's as fucked up as you or similarly fucked up. You then have to navigate the similar fuck-ups, and that is work, hard work. Couples who've been together for a long time will exclaim proudly, actually boast, of how they've navigated the other person's fucked-up mannerisms and gained equal understanding of mutual fucked-up behavior. They endure, with satisfaction and bickering, each other's fucked-up ways.

Now apply this to a single person in the dating menagerie. As we grow older our patience for another person's fucked-up mannerisms gradually erodes. With each passing week you try to endure the other's fucked-up behavior as they try to navigate yours. You ask yourself, are they more fucked up than someone else? Was that fuck-up really worth trying it for another week, a month, or a lifetime? Are their fucked-up traits tolerable for eternity? Can I change their fucked-up behavior to jell with my fucked-up behavior, or do I need to change my fucked-up behavior?

The questions repeat endlessly, but ever so slowly fade into acceptance. Eventually, you look forward to sharing your life and growing old with that other similarly fucked-up person. And so you finally become a couple repeating, adjusting, or correcting past fucked-up characteristics and behaviors. When things get too fucked up between you two, you ask the Divine for help and everything seems to be all right again. You become a loving couple as you might have once been with someone else a long short time ago.

Chapter Fourteen

Divinity, Part Two — The Signs

DURING THE SPRING BEFORE Hope's cancer returned, she and I experienced the best time, post-children, in our married life. We firmly believed that the cancer was eradicated. The years of chemotherapy had taught us to treasure each other once again. We had reinvented our intimacy and it was flourishing. We discovered common interests and started to pursue them with vigor.

One was a newfound spirituality and the urge to discover what it was. We'd both given up religion but felt extremely close to the Divine. In the spring, we traveled to Utah and stayed in a resort near Snow Canyon State Park. We hiked the park almost every day, discovering the natural wonders of stone, fauna, and flora. One morning, we hired a Native American spiritualist to lead us on an ethereal journey. He brought us to a place of intense vortex energy and commenced our spiritual exploration playing a Native American flute. If you're not aware of the sound, the flute sings a melody that you often hear during a massage, yoga, or meditation session.

As he played, the chanting sound of the flute gripped my soul. Not a grip of pain or sorrow but one of an internal, intense divine feeling—the type of feeling you get only a few times in life and know it's something rare and special. I had to learn to play the flute. I had to possess one. I had to master the instrument and let it guide my life. The experience with the spiritualist was profound, and I'll reserve description of it for another time, but the flute was the message from it.

After many trials and errors in buying flutes, I was rewarded with one made by Michael Graham Allen, known as Coyote Oldman. His flute felt like an extension of my spirituality and Divinity. A short time after I'd been rewarded with Michael's flute, Hope's cancer returned. A very dangerous and difficult surgical ordeal fell upon us, which endured for well over three months. Hope's hospital room at Mt. Sinai Hospital in New York City, overlooked Central Park, and the park was where I refined my flute-playing skills. I played that flute every evening, every weekend, and prior to every operation and procedure as Hope's agony unfolded. With each day's practice, music started to come out of the flute, replacing missed notes and screeching noise. The flute inspired us, and especially me, with the energy, the courage, and the means to persevere through the daily medical onslaught. The flute was an extension of the Divine. It was a gift from the Divine given to us at Snow Canyon State Park. The Divine knew we would need Michael's flute to endure and survive this new episode. Our comprehension of this sign, this gift, was realized a short while after the rabbi shared his words of wisdom with us during our worst day in the hospital. On that day, I carried the flute in my hand to play it in Central Park. The flute was one of many signs to be revealed, just as the rabbi foretold.

Hope had never fully recovered after the infection and her long hospital stay. The precise progression from cancer to wellness back to cancer is blurred with chronological confusion. I do know our intimacy never fully returned, and it became nonexistent for months and at times, years. I tried hard to remain true to my vows. I complained to a number of friends about my sexual frustration. A friend approached me and said, "You've been the best a man can be. But I know of a place that's extremely discrete and clean should you want to have intercourse again." I thanked him and said I would think about it. The idea of intercourse with another woman, after decades of monogamy, was emotionally disruptive.

After a week or so I called my friend and said yes. We arranged an evening. The days leading up to it were fraught with inner disruptions of conscience. I awoke the morning of the interlude and smelled breakfast. This was common on weekends, but on weekdays Hope never woke up before I did and made me breakfast. That morning, as always, I awoke at 5:15, having set aside my clothes the night before, so Hope could sleep past my leaving.

But this morning of my planned breaking of our vows, I smelled eggs, turkey bacon, and toast. Hope was undergoing intense chemo treatments. She slept late into the mornings. I asked, "Why did you get up to make me breakfast?"

She answered, "I just felt the urge, and I appreciate all you've been doing for me."

I remembered the rabbi's words and canceled my evening plans. Hope never again made me breakfast on a weekday morning.

My friend, Scotty, was a constant mess with women. Hope counseled him frequently to ease his struggles. After Hope's death, Scotty began to turn his life around. During dinner one evening he described his troubles and opportunities. As he talked I felt Hope's strong presence next to me, the kind of presence you feel when you enter a dark room and the hair on your back stands up as if someone were there with you. Hope filled my mind with these words: "Tell Scotty all will be fine."

And so I relayed, "Scotty, all will be fine. Trust me." I never revealed where the thought came from. Scotty looked confused. Several minutes later he confided in me.

"Dennis," he said, "You'll think I'm crazy, but I just saw Hope sitting next to you!"

This was one of two episodes in which Scotty and I experienced Hope together. Just as Hope foreshadowed, Scotty found his life partner. He is now living a fulfilled life.

Ten months before Hope passed, our second home in the Berkshires burned down. Nothing remained. A friend and I watched as the home disappeared. At first the fire was small, and only about 15 percent of the home was damaged. Then, after we all thought the destruction was done, a fierce wind blew out of the north and fanned the embers until a raging fire erupted. As the fire raged, one of the firemen broke the fire hydrant. In addition, the fire department couldn't draw water from the frozen lake near our home.

I watched for almost an hour as no water poured out of the hoses and the fire slowly consumed the home in a horizontal, windblown fashion. The flames danced on my frustration as my dream home faded away.

Six weeks after the fire, Hope's cancer returned, and a different dream started to burn away. Four weeks after that, the cancer invaded her bones, which was extremely rare for ovarian cancer. My life was falling apart with hers. The years of caregiving and running a construction division during this intense emotional time took their toll on me. I left work reassured that the insurance money I got from the fire damage would provide temporary financial stability. The stars then seemed to align, and we lived out Hope's last months with greater peace. For the first time in my life I had no occupational worries and could tend to my family. After Hope died I decided to rebuild the home. It was my sanctuary from the hustle and bustle of New York City construction life. I regretted Hope not being a part of it, but her decorating lessons helped me redesign and furnish the home. I went there a lot. Early one morning I went upstairs to the meditation area I had recreated. It had elements of our first home in it. Around my wrist was a yellow yarn I had tied there shortly after Hope's death. The path of the yarn from Hope's prayer altar to my wrist is also a Divinely inspired story; I'll share it with you if we ever meet. As I meditated the string was tugged, I mean *tugged*—not once but twice. The tug was like the initial tug from a caught fish. I was startled and scared. I tried to envision a realistic cause for the tug, but I couldn't. Something, someone, had tugged at that string. And then, after I regained composure, a revelation dawned: The house had burned down for two reasons: So I could quit work and tend to Hope and my family for the last months of her life with no monetary fears; and because I wouldn't have kept the original Otis, Massachusetts, home but would have sold it and moved away. How could I share our dream home with another woman? But the new home was one that Hope never set foot in. I could share that new home with another life mate. We could build our own dreams together, not the dreams Hope and I had shared. Hope had tugged that string. Hope had given me her approval to build a new life. After that incident, her visitations became less frequent and have all but disappeared as I finish this story.

Postscript

SEPTEMBER 2013, ROUGHLY A year and half after Hope died, my friend Joan called me and said there was someone she'd like me to meet. I agreed and met the woman after work. My first meeting with Lisa took place on the steps of USS *Maine* National Monument near Columbus Circle in Manhattan. As I approached her, I was taken aback. She wasn't my image of the women I usually dated, who were short and small-framed. She wore business-like attire, was four or more inches taller than I, and was elegant and extremely attractive. I was a little discomfited by her appearance, because I felt she was out of my league, and sized her up mistakenly without saying hello.

Our date was at times awkward and at times comfortable. As the evening neared its end I wasn't sure a second date was likely, but my friend Lori's words echoed in my mind. Lori was a widow who married a man named Harry. Lori's first date with him was just okay, but her friend urged her to go on a second date. Because of this, Lori always guided me to go on two dates with a person.

With Lori's philosophy well planted, I decided to kiss Lisa good-bye as she entered a Yellow Taxi to go home. I kissed her not once but twice. Lisa had pretty much decided she wasn't going to see me again, but the kiss, not a serpent's kiss, but a normal, sincere kiss, planted a question in her mind about seeing me again. The kiss, along with her youngest daughter's urging, sent her for a second meeting with me.

I guess all my lessons from all my dates and all my men's magazine articles paid off. We went on a second date and a third and a fourth, and we now live together, building a new life. Lisa was patient and understanding of my sexual recovery needs. Lisa was the woman who put the pillow under my head and told me "no pressure" during our first lovemaking session. My Ego Penis returned and I was acting like a teenager again in bed—yeah, baby! Together, Lisa and I scuba dive, snow ski, hike glaciers to beaches, play ice hockey, work out, snowshoe.... Richie, it is a possible dream. Lisa and I are in the same business, and we talk for hours on end about work and every conceivable subject. She challenges me in sports and in life with a loving fervor that expands our universe in all directions. Lisa loves my body hair and winces at the thought of any of it being removed; her fingers groom my chest hairs with affection. And the best is that Lisa and I are mingling families, pasts, and futures. We're sharing and helping each other's families recover from years of misfortune and tears. Are those moments, as described in *Blade Runner,* lost in time like tears in the rain, or are they really the tears of a new beginning that we just don't comprehend during the tumultuous storm?

Oh, and for the Divine and its signs, Joan shared a Divine sign with us several months later. Before asking Lisa if she wanted to meet me, Joan observed a white glow hovering over Lisa's head like a halo. It was this Divine glow that inspired Joan to ask Lisa about meeting me. Was it Hope who placed the halo? Was it the Divine, or just a bright lighting fixture above, casting the glow on Lisa? *Ask the rabbi—he might know.*

Life is evolving for me. Lisa is great, and I couldn't ask for a better new soulmate. I just feel so bad that Hope could not enjoy this time in life. She made me such a good person, and enabled me to lead a better life and create a new type of relationship the second time around. Our marriage was great, but it could have been so much better—like regrets from high school. Four years after Hope's death,

I still cry for the wonderful, joyous memories of our life together. Those tears will never stop flowing from my eyes. I cry for the future the Divine has offered. Grief can bring joy. We just need to learn how to embrace and trust the process. It's the Divine's intention that we learn to live life. Thank you for letting me share *Love, Loss, and Awakening* with you.

> *"Be led by your dreams … not driven by your fears."*
> — *Betty Hill Crowson*

About the Author

DENNIS P. FREED IS a native of Brooklyn, New York, and grew up in Oceanside, Long Island, where he later raised his family. He earned a BS in Civil Engineering at the University of Rhode Island. After a stint as a structural engineer, he entered the Construction Management and Development profession in New York City where he has led teams to construct and develop over sixty-five buildings. Also a visiting professor at Pratt University in New York, he teaches Construction Management to architecture students. When he's not writing, Dennis enjoys ice hockey, model railroading, hiking, skiing, scuba diving, and playing Native American flutes.

RESOURCES

ALLEN, MICHAEL GRAHAM. Crafts ancient flutes of North America and is the composer of Coyote Oldman music, http://coyoteoldman.com/

BRADEN, GREGG. *The Divine Matrix: Bridging Time, Space, Miracles and Belief.* Hay House, January 2008.

CHAPMAN, GARY D. *The 5 Love Languages: The Secret to Love that Lasts.*

CROWSON, BETTY HILL. *The Busy Person's Guide to Balance and Boundaries.* AuthorHouse, December 2013.

CROWSON, BETTY HILL. *The Joy Is In the Journey: A Woman's Guide Through Crisis and Change.* AuthorHouse, April 25, 2005.

DUFF, MICHAEL AND MICHAEL GREEN. *Nova-The Elegant Universe.* PBS January 2004.

FREED, DENNIS. www.lovelossandawakening.com

HENDRIX, HARVILLE, Ph.D. and HELEN LAKELLY HUNT, Ph. D. *Getting The Love You Want.*

KRIPALU CENTER FOR YOGA AND HEALTH. Stockbridge, Mass.

Men's Health Magazine. Rodale Publishing.

NEW YORK OPEN CENTER. New York, NY.

NOLFI, GEORGE. *The Adjustment Bureau.* Universal Studios, June 2011.

ROSENBLUM, BRUCE AND FRED KUTTNER. *Quantum Enigma: Physics Encounters Consciousness.* Oxford University Press, August 2011.

ROSENTHAL, SHERI. *The Complete Idiot's Guide to Toltec Wisdom.* alpha, September 2005.

RUIZ, DON MIGUEL. *The Four Agreements: A Practical Guide to Personal Freedom.* Amber-Allen Publishing, November 1997.

SCOTT, RIDLEY. *Blade Runner* (30th Anniversary Collector's Edition). Warner Home Video, October 2012.

THORNE, KIP, *The Science of Interstellar.* W. W. Norton & Company, November 2014.

WOMAN TO WOMAN, Support and mentoring to women undergoing gynecologic cancers; Mount Sinai Hospital, http://www.mountsinai.org/patient-care/service-areas/obgyn-and-reproductive-services/patient-support-services/womens-gynecologic-cancer-support/women-to-women-program

CPSIA information can be obtained
at www.ICGtesting.com
Printed in the USA
FFOW02n0623020616
24516FF